Imagine!

Enhancing Your

Problem-Solving

and Critical

Thinking Skills

By **Anthony D. Paustian**

Illustrated by Michael D. Paustian

Foreword by Dr. John Huntley

Prentice Hall
Upper Saddle River, NJ 07458

Library of Congress Cataloging-in-Publication Data
Paustian, Anthony D.,
    Imagine! : enhancing your problem-solving and critical thinking
skills / by Anthony D. Paustian.
        p.   cm.
    Includes bibliographical references (p, 176).
    ISBN 0-13-234808-X (alk. paper)
    1. Problem solving--Handbooks, manuals, etc. 2. Creative
thinking--Handbooks, manuals, etc.   I. Title.
    HD30.29.P38   1997
    153.4'3--dc20   96-10344
                                                        CIP

Acquisitions Editor: *Elizabeth Sugg*
Production Editor: *Denise Brown*
Director of Manufacturing & Production: *Bruce Johnson*
Manufacturing Buyer: *Ed O'Dougherty*
Editorial Assistant: *Kahdijah Bell*
Formatting/page make-up: *Anthony D. Paustian*
Printer/Binder: *Banta Harrisonburg*

©1997 by Prentice-Hall, Inc.
A Simon & Schuster Company
Upper Saddle River, New Jersey 07458

Printed in the United States of America

10   9   8   7   6   5   4   3   2   1

ISBN 0-13-234808-X

Prentice-Hall International (UK) Limited, *London*
Prentice-Hall of Australia Pty. Limited, *Sydney*
Prentice-Hall Canada Inc., *Toronto*
Prentice-Hall Hispanoamericana, S.A., *Mexico*
Prentice-Hall of India Private Limited, *New Delhi*
Prentice-Hall of Japan, Inc., *Tokyo*
Simon & Schuster Asia Pte. Ltd., *Singapore*
Editora Prentice-Hall do Brasil, Ltda., *Rio de Janeiro*

Table of Contents.

Table of Contents

To **Nese**, and the kid in all of us.

Foreword

Foreword.

If you let this little book get to you, a lot of things will start to happen. The world won't be any different, but you will see connections where none appeared before. Before, it was fragments. Now, it's new wholes. You will start thinking of yourself as a creative person and team player. Your world will feel less like a prison (other people's rules) and more like a playground (your own rules).

That's quite a lot to claim for a little book of good advice. The secret, of course, hides with the "if": "If you let this book get hold of you . . . ."

Imagine! is really about making connections. And the author makes it relatively painless for you to begin connecting. As you read, you will feel connected to a timeless universe of other writers and thinkers because nearly every page brings you a bonus quotation, just a phrase, maybe a sentence or two, that puts your reading into a wider, deeper context. These are the echoes that roll across centuries, giving strangers the power to recognize each other.

You will also feel connected to a specialized world of scholars and their research because Mr. Paustian cites the authorities, quotes their books, acknowledges their help, and then extends, applies, reshapes, and connects familiar ideas into new contexts of problem solving, decision making, team working, and quality choosing.

Soon, you will start feeling new connections internally because this edition of *Imagine!* adds exercises after each chapter. They come in three flavors, and the pattern repeats: first, a personal inventory of experience, thoughts, and feelings, "who are you, where have you been, what have you seen, and what do you want?"; second, some puzzle problems to be solved; and finally, a journal in which to record the stages of your continuing journey.

Oh yeah, great, wow, wahoo, and who's going to actually do all this? Well, that's the problem with a lot of these self-help books, But wait, **Imagine!** is not a self-help book (although you could use it that way if you had more will power than most of us). It's actually a textbook, an old-fashioned textbook, like for reading in school. Yes? It's designed to focus the work of studious people (what they're studying is creativity) under the guidance of a teacher. And here's where the last set of connections come in, the really important ones. These are the connections from you outward toward other people: interpersonal, social, and finally political.

As the blind poet, Homer, prayed to his Muse at the beginning of *The Odyssey*, that epic tale of coming home, finally, after much wandering about: "Make this tale live for us in all its many bearings, Oh Muse."

Dr. John Huntley, Ph.D.
Professor of English Literature, University of Iowa

Preface

Preface.

The rewards in life—school grades, praise from our parents and peers, and job performance raises and bonuses—have usually come from following the rules and getting the "right" answers, rather than examining problems from many angles and exploring many answers. As we enter into a global marketplace and economy, it is becoming increasingly evident that our society, including the educational and business sectors, can no longer follow this same pattern of rewards if we are to survive as a superior nation.

Rather, it will be through creative problem solving and the teaching of creativity techniques within our varying problem-solving environments that we as a society will be able to succeed in the workplace of the 21st century. However, have creativity and the teaching of techniques to foster creative thinking been included as part of our present educational structure, both formal or otherwise?

Although there has been approximately a 500% increase in creativity training in industry in the last few years, only about a forth of that training has appeared at large companies such as MCI Telecommunications, Frito-Lay, Inc., Dupont, and General Electric. Some colleges and universities have also added creativity and problem-solving courses to their required curriculum, but only a very small percentage.

In an era of intense competition from national to global, fresh ideas have become the most precious of raw materials in our development. It is the purpose of this book to explore creativity and the problem-solving process and the extent to which it is part of our educational process.

notes

ACKNOWLEDGMENTS.

I am particularly indebted to Dr. Ray Muston and Dr. John Huntley who, through their support, demands and mutual respect, instilled into me a drive to apply all that I have learned and to share that knowledge with others. My sincere appreciation also goes to a number of people who, through their reviews, helped make this book possible. Through the insight and helpful suggestions of John Wiltbank and Carolyn Curtis, I was empowered to further develop and enhance this book by keeping focused on its vision. Thanks to Andrea Worrell who opened my eyes towards the clarity of its purpose. And finally, a special word of gratitude goes to the administration of the American Institute of Commerce for allowing me to utilize this book in a classroom environment during its initial stages.

How to Use This Book.

Creativity is like a sport. When you are trying to excel at a particular sport, it takes considerable practice and work to master the necessary skills. Just going to scheduled practice sessions alone will not be enough. You must continually practice, practice, and practice to ultimately master the skills and hence, the sport.

Therefore, this book should be viewed as a tool, and as such, should be used as both a guide and handbook to help yourself practice some of the methods and techniques necessary to open up your creative thinking skills. Like with mastering a sport, creative thinking also takes practice. Simply attending a class or reading this or any other book on the subject will not be enough.

This is an organic text which will grow as you grow. As such, all work, notes, and ideas that are accomplished while using this book should remain in the book. There is substantial space in the left column of each page and in the additional workspace section located at the back of this text for note taking, spontaneous sketching, doodling, brainwriting, mindmapping, and just about anything else for that matter. To help open up and stimulate the visual side of your brain, the illustrations in the book were done in such a way so as to encourage "coloring" and personal modification. In some places within the text, a blank space exists entitled "Draw Picture." Within this space, you are encouraged to draw your own illustrations to coincide with how you interpret the text at that point.

I hope you will find this book both useful and exciting. Have a ball!!!

1
Creativity Defined

Creativity Defined.

Creativity is basically the production of order out of chaos. It is knowing without knowing or conscious reasoning. It is belief without evidence (Ray and Myers, 1986). This definition has been cited on many occasions by Asian philosophers to their students, but what does it mean? As logic-driven people, we may have a difficult time in grasping the true essence of its meaning. Therefore, we will begin our focus by developing an understanding of the brain and where creativity comes from.

The Brain.

As a result of Roger Sperry's brain studies in the 1960s in which he and his associate Michael S. Gazzaniga won the Nobel Prize, it was discovered that the brain is comprised of two distinct hemispheres. Each hemisphere has its own specialized set of traits which are detailed as follows:

> **LEFT BRAIN:** Verbal (language), logical, number-oriented, sequential, looks at details, linear, symbolic representation, judgmental, analytical, rigid, practical, rational, concrete, scientific
>
> **RIGHT BRAIN:** Visual (images), musical (rhythm), imaginative, color, holistic, pattern-oriented, emotional, nonjudgmental, conceptual, spiritual, playful, flexible

> *"It may be that the only limits to the human mind are those we believe in . . . but those are extremely powerful"* - *Willis Harmon*

2

Chapter 1 Creativity Defined.

Within the last few years, the term "Right-Brained" has become a faddish way of saying creative, artistic, and "neat" as opposed to the supposedly dull, analytical, stolid opposite, "Left-Brained" (Wycoff, 1991). The unfortunate result of this abbreviated, simplistic way of looking at people is the misconception that a person is either "Right-Brained" or "Left-Brained," when in reality both sides of our brain and their respective traits are critical to our thinking processes. Creativity results from the extraordinary interaction between both hemispheres of the brain rather than being a product of the right hemisphere only. To begin the creative process, we must actively engage both hemispheres of our brains.

Ned Herrmann (1991), author of *The Creative Brain*, divides the brain into four distinct sections or quadrants each having its own characteristics. Along with the left brain, or left cerebral hemisphere, and the right brain, or right cerebral hemisphere, he also includes the central limbic system which he divided into two halves, the left

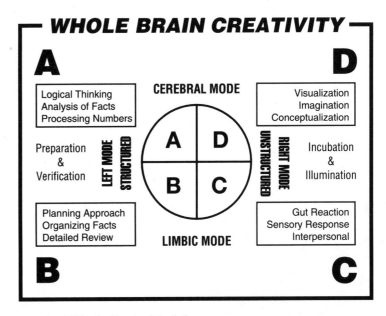

Figure 1A - Whole Brain Model

limbic and the right limbic, both endowed with a cortex capable of thinking and connected by a connecting joint—just like the cerebral hemispheres. This four-quadrant or whole brain model is illustrated in Figure 1A. The cerebral hemispheres are the location of cognitive and intellectual functions, while the limbic system is focused on effect and emotion. These functions include organizing and transforming information for processing, as well as the emotional elements of learning. His whole brain model is not a physiological map but a metaphor for whole brain thinking. The creative thought process is a counterclockwise move through the four thought process quadrants A, B, C & D and the two categories, structured (left) and unstructured (right). The whole brain model is dependent on all four quadrants, being situationally available during all four phases of the creative process. Quadrants A and D represent the more cognitive and intellectual processes associated with the two cerebral hemispheres, while Quadrants B and C represent the emotional processes associated with the limbic system. If one quadrant is closed down, creative potential is diminished. If two or more quadrants are closed down, then applied creativity as a desired outcome ceases. The process stops. Synergy, which means that the whole is greater than the sum of its parts, is denied.

Using his model, Herrmann describes a typical breakthrough act which shows that full creative functioning is a basic human capability.

Consider two people: one, a high-ranking military officer who strongly prefers

analytical, quantitative, factual modes of thinking and dismisses the emotional, interpersonal, intuitive approaches (loves A, avoids C); the other, a music therapist who strongly prefers insightful, intuitive, feeling, and sensing modes and avoids, even shys away from, rational processing (loves C, avoids A).

Their assignment is to solve a problem together. The statement of the problem includes numerous facts, many quantifiable, but not enough to lead one to any logical conclusion. Missing elements and gaps in the data call for more than strictly linear problem solving.

The ways in which these two approach the problem reflect their extreme preferences. The army officer, with intense A quadrant preferences, quantifies the elements of the problem and pushes for a mathematical solution. The music therapist, on the other hand, feels frightened by all the facts and data and can't understand what the officer is doing. As he works, she moves away to a place near the window, where she ponders the problem while looking out into the garden. After the preliminary discussion, no one speaks for 10 or 15 minutes. Then, when the colonel is on the third page of his mathematical treatment, the young woman turns to him and says, "I've got it." He responds, "What do you mean, you've got it?" She says, "I don't know how to describe the answer, but I know it's right." "What do you mean, you know it's right? And how can I tell what it is if you can't even describe it?" "I can draw it for you," she replies. Taking some crayons, she draws some symbols representing the elements of the problem and the relationship between them.

"Okay, I see that," he admits, "but I don't see the solution." She then says, "Well, let me show you," and proceeds to move her body in one way to express one aspect of the problem and then in another way to express another aspect. And then, again, through movement, she shows how these two elements come together to form a solution. The colonel is dumbfounded, because she has indeed grasped the answer.

The assignment calls for a report to the group, and the colonel says, "Since you got the answer, you give the report." The woman replies, "There's no way I can explain what I just demonstrated." Whereupon, the colonel answers, "Well, I still don't know how in the world you did it, but I'm satisfied that you did do it and I can explain not only what you did, but why it's the right answer."

Returning to the group, he articulates both the problem-solving process and the answer. Awed, the music therapist exclaims, "My goodness, that's wonderful! Teach me how to do that." Smiling, the army colonel responds, "I will, but only if you teach me how to do what you did."

What these two individuals learned was that one's best style can be enhanced by adding a style one discounts or even fears. As a result, both people reordered their value systems and priorities to accommodate and develop styles of thinking that they deprecated and avoided for most of their adult lives (Herrmann, 1991).

As in the story of the army colonel and music therapist, the truly creative person needs to recognize that effective thinking involves both a logical, sequential frame of mind and a creative, generative one. In other words, for one to be highly creative, whole brain thinking must occur.

Edward de Bono (1990) resolves this apparent contradiction in  the two halves of the brain by identifying two kinds of thinking: vertical and lateral. Vertical thinking, often called logical or traditional thinking, is the type of thinking that most people are familiar with. This type of thinking tends to follow sequential patterns, working step by step toward the best solution to a problem. Vertical thinking is concerned with rightness, and to proceed correctly, an individual needs to be certain that each step on the path towards a solution is a correct step. Thus, vertical thinking requires people to make judgments and to determine whether a step is right or wrong. In sharp contrast, lateral thinking is associated with humor, insight, and what the average person would call "creativity." The thought process tends to follow the least likely path and is often provocative versus reactive. Lateral thinking continually challenges

notes

_____

_____

_____

_____

_____

_____

_____

_____

_____

_____

_____

_____

_____

_____

_____

_____

_____

_____

_____

_____

_____

"Every individual is a marvel of unknown and unrealized possibilities."
- Goethe

accepted methods and principles. This type of thinking suspends judgement and bias. It is exploring, generates numerous ideas, and experiments with different solutions to solving problems. Vertical and lateral thinking are partners rather than opponents. Therefore, we need to be aware of both types of thinking and how to use them simultaneously in order to solve problems effectively.

Creative Skills and Traits.

Creativity is both a process and a capability. As a process it is the production of something that is not made by ordinary means. As a capability, it consists of three general elements: fluency, flexibility, and originality. *Fluency* is the ability to create many solutions for a particular problem with the emphasis being on quantity rather than quality. *Flexibility* is the ability to shift thinking from one type into other types of thinking. *Originality* is the ability to overcome traditional ways of thinking to produce new connections thereby creating new solutions to problems (Macaranas, 1982).

Torrance and Ball (1984) describe five creativity skills. These skills will be explained in depth in later chapters.

- ORIGINALITY—
  Originality is
  the ability to
  make new
  combinations
  of elements, to
  break away
  from the
  obvious.

Draw Picture

n o t e s

- FLUENCY——Fluency is the ability to generate many ideas to solve the same problem. (Brainstorming is the best method to use—See Chapter 4.)

- ABSTRACTING——Abstracting is the ability to zoom in on the true essence of the situation or problem. It is the ability to identify the most effective and efficient solution from a number of possibilities. (Effective and efficient goal attainment—See Chapter 6.)

- ELABORATION——Elaboration is the ability to make an idea usable by fanning it out into detail and specifics. (Planning —See Chapter 7.)

- OPENNESS——Openness is the ability to resist premature judgement and bias. It allows for many solutions to a single problem. (Ask & Listen—See Chapter 5.)

The creative person not only exhibits these five skills, but also has become conscious of his or her own thinking process. By utilizing these five skills, the creative person becomes aware of the activities involved in thinking, thereby encouraging individuals to carefully examine the steps they follow to solve problems as well as the methods they use while thinking.

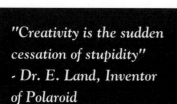

Too often people, when discussing creativity, refer to the works of great artists or inventors—the paintings of Picasso, the music of Beethoven, the inventions of Edison or Newton, the

n o t e s

architecture of Wright, the theories of Einstein—and although these people did display extraordinary creativity and talent, creativity is in all of us. It is simply a matter of seeing things that everyone else sees while making CONNECTIONS that no one else has made. Connection-making is the ability to draw from a variety of sources, pull this information together, and synthesize it into a new whole. As a result, new meaning is brought to a purpose or task, an existing problem is solved, or beauty or value is added to something existing.

For example, Fred Smith, founder of Federal Express, created the method of overnight shipping by making a connection with how the Federal Reserve clears checks. All checks within a given region are sent by individual banks to a central clearinghouse where they are sorted and then sent back to the bank on which the checks were drawn. Learning this process while in college, Smith made the connection with shipping packages in a similar manner. A package being sent from Chicago to Detroit would first have to be flown to a central clearinghouse which, in the case of Federal Express, is located in Memphis, Tennessee. On the surface, it may seem absurd to send a package from Chicago to Detroit by way of Memphis. However, as the success of Federal Express has shown, the connection was not only creative, but a good one.

Draw Picture

Other examples of real-life connections include Newton

connecting the falling apple to gravity, Watt connecting the steam kettle to the invention of the steam engine, da Vinci connecting the ringing of a church bell which occurred at the same time he threw a rock into the water with the understanding of sound waves, Colt connecting a ship's wheel with the invention of the revolver, and Diesel connecting a typewriter with the invention of the Diesel engine. In his book entitled 99% *Inspiration*, Bryan Mattimore calls these real-world objects and occurrences "Idea Hooks®" which become symbols for anything you want them to be.

Creative people have an abundance of imagination. They tend to get very involved in the problem or task at hand and can easily become totally absorbed in it. They seem to be almost childlike in their vitality, curiosity, and enthusiasm. Children tend to have boundless energy to explore, search, and dream, and are very passionate in their approach to the serious business of play (Ferrett, 1994).

Since each of us has unique perspectives, different talents, and varying experiences, creativity becomes a matter of turning this base into something tangible within some specified context whether it be management, production, art, music, engineering, school, or anything else. It is important to remember that the most important aspect of creativity is realizing that it does not necessarily come from having one right answer. There are many, many solutions to any problem and many, many problems to most solutions.

However, a good problem solver knows how important it is to guard against wishful thinking, biased attitudes, misperception, and other distortions to his or her thinking. When you get stuck or are overwhelmed by the problem facing you, you can draw upon the same

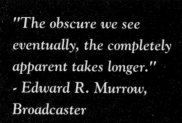

"The obscure we see eventually, the completely apparent takes longer."
- Edward R. Murrow, Broadcaster

n o t e s

creative resources and problem-solving methods each time to expand your awareness and open up new possibilities and alternatives (Ferrett, 1994). What are the traits of a creative person? The majority of studies and research indicate seven traits as being common to most creative people:

- COURAGE—Creative people are willing to endeavor into new areas and are willing to risk failure (which to them is simply a learning experience and something new to overcome).

- SELF-EXPRESSION—Creative people are not afraid to express their thoughts and feelings. They are willing to be themselves at all times.

- HUMOR—Humor is closely related to creativity. When elements are combined in a way that is different, unexpected, and fun, we end up with humor. Many new and useful combinations have begun with humor.

- INTUITION — Intuition is a state of knowing without conscious reasoning (Ray & Myers, 1986). Creative people accept their intuition as a legitimate part of their thinking. They understand that much intuition comes from the right brain versus the left brain which does not communicate in the same manner.

- CURIOSITY—Creative people have a natural desire to know everything about anything. They know that at any given time,

unexpected connections might be made, giving rise to a new idea.

- **DRIVE TO QUESTION**—Creative people constantly ask such questions as "why?" "why not?" "should?" "could?"
- **PERSISTENCE**—Creative people know the importance of sticking with a problem and working it through. If not, a solution or brilliant idea may never be found.

Other traits which I have observed include playfulness, independence, flexibility, and a high level of motivation. Creative people also seem to have a diverse background with a large, broad level of accumulated knowledge which assists in the connection-making process.

Creativity is a personal process. It thrives at all levels and in all phases of a person's being. It is also a skill and therefore requires practice. Like a sport, just going to scheduled practices once in a while will not be enough to master the necessary skills. You must continually practice, practice, and practice to ultimately master the skills of creativity and make it part of your everyday thinking. Although each of us is equally creative, it sometimes comes easier to some people than to others.

Painter Stanley A. Czurles believes we suffer from a case of "spectatoritis" which leads to increased feelings of worthlessness, lack of satisfaction, and apathy. Some symptoms of spectatoritis include bouts of boredom, a lack of personal challenge, too much "free" time, pessimism, limited success, and short-term satisfaction. On the other hand, the creative person is involved in self-enriching activities, strives to achieve new goals, maintains flexibility in thinking, and keeps a youthful spirit while applying the various techniques to

n o t e s

enhance creativity (Grupas, 1990).

"What I wish it could be" is far more important than "what is." Many corporations understand the power of this concept as they take great pains to develop and communicate their corporate vision. As discussed in the next section, a constant sense of creative awareness must be instilled into each person with the process beginning in our educational system. It has been said that the

Brain Calisthenics

only constant in life is change. People must be taught to see alternatives instead of searching for the "one right answer," to envision the consequences and results for each decision, to weigh the risk-reward trade-off with each choice, and then realize that in time due to change, the chosen solution may no longer be viable. Creativity in problem solving is not a destination, it is an ongoing journey. In essence, it is like solving a jigsaw puzzle with no set conclusion but instead an infinite number of possibilities.

Questions for Discussion.

1. List some of the characteristics specific to each hemisphere of the brain. Using this list, describe which list you associate yourself with the most and why? _____

_____

_____

_____

_____

_____

_____

_____

_____

_____

2. List the characteristics of creative people. After looking at this list, describe what areas you feel you can strongly associate with and those you cannot. Cite reasons for your beliefs._____

_____

_____

_____

_____

_____

_____

_____

_____

_____

_____

3. List some ways in which you may suffer from "spectatoritis." What do you feel to be the cause(s) of these feelings? _____

_____

_____

_____

_____

_____

_____

_____

_____

Exercises.

 Connect all nine dots with no more than four connecting lines without lifting your pen. Try for more than one solution.

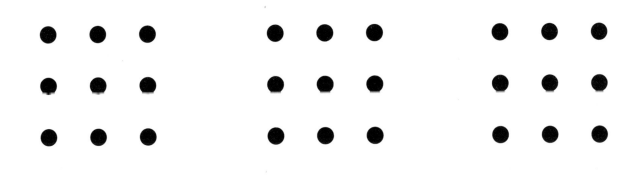

 It is easy to arrange nine checkers in eight rows of three checkers each, but harder to arrange nine checkers in ten rows of three checkers each. Do both. How about nine checkers in six rows of three checkers each? Nine checkers in seven rows of three checkers each?

1C In your own words, write a definition for the word laughter and draw a picture representing it.

_____

_____

_____

Exercises.

Journal. Starting with this chapter, begin keeping a journal of your ideas, feelings, thoughts, dreams, occurrences, how you felt about this chapter, or just about anything else for that matter. As will be discussed later in the book, ideas will come spontaneously to you. Research shows that if an idea is not written down within 24 hours of it occurring, it will most likely be lost. You should get in the habit of keeping a daily journal. You will never know if that great idea for tomorrow just came to you today. Additional writing space will be provided at the end of each chapter.

Becoming Creative

Becoming Creative.

For many years conventional wisdom was that you were either creative (imaginative, wild, hard to manage, and entrepreneurial) or you were not (logical, organized, and not particularly innovative). Today research demonstrates that almost anyone can learn to develop his or her innate creativity.

Creativity is not a talent; it is a way of operating, a mode of behaving. The most creative people have simply acquired an ability for getting themselves into a particular mood—a way of operating—which allows their creative abilities to develop and expand (Cleese, 1991). Creativity seems to blossom for many people when they are doing something new, something that is forcing them to grow in all parts of their life (Ray, 1986). The environment is important too. It is much easier to solve problems in a creative climate where new ideas are welcomed than in an environment that will not tolerate failure or divergent approaches to problem solving.

Many people believe that they are not skilled enough in a particular area; thus they do not have the expertise necessary to be creative. Remember that the ballpoint pen was invented by a sculptor and the parking meter by a journalist. A musician developed Kodachrome film while the automatic telephone was produced by an undertaker. The pneumatic tire was developed by a veterinarian (Grupas, 1990). Being creative is everyone's business.

Inner Self.

To become creative, however, one must discover their inner self and translate it into unique outward actions. In the early 1950s, Abraham Maslow developed a framework that helps explain the strength of certain needs. From his research, he seemed to find a hierarchy into which human needs arrange themselves. This pyramid-shaped model, or "hierarchy of needs," has basic physiological needs at the bottom and the need for self-actualization at the top (see Figure 2A). Before higher-order needs (esteem and self-actualization) are activated, certain lower-order needs (physiological, safety, and social/love) must be satisfied. Discovering one's inner self to enhance creative behavior is found at the self-actualization level. According to Maslow, a self-actualized person is

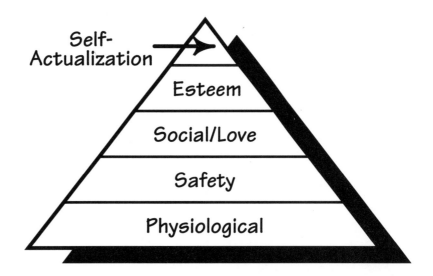

Maslow's Hierarchy of Needs

Figure 2A

n o t e s

one who is striving to fulfill his or her potential using all of their capabilities. He or she is trying to become everything that he or she is capable of becoming. In his research, he found that self-actualized people have several characteristic traits:

- Is original and inventive with a fresh perspective and simple yet direct way of viewing life

- Tends to do most activities creatively, but does not necessarily possess any outstanding talent; can take or leave connections

- Has an accurate and objective perception of reality; is not frightened by the unknown and enjoys ambiguity

- Is problem-centered, not self-centered; has a purpose in life

- Accepts him or herself and human nature for what it is

- Is forthright, spontaneous, and genuine

- Has a strong, thoughtful sense of humor that is constructive, not destructive; loves life and has zest in living; can handle stress and is resilient

- Needs time alone more so than others so as to concentrate

- Has a drive towards independence, autonomy, and self-sufficiency; has less need for praise and recognition

- Has an awareness of "peak experiences"—moments of heightened pleasure

- Is very ethical and moral; strives towards some futuristic vision; enjoys setting goals as well as the work required in achieving the goals

- Is capable of removing him or herself from society and culture and able to view them objectively

- Tends to be benevolent, considerate, and unselfish

- Develops close relationships with relatively few people, but is capable of a greater love
(Maslow, 1954, 1962)

"Capacities clamor to be used and cease their clamor only when they are well used."
- A.H. Maslow

Chapter 2   Becoming Creative.

Developing self-actualization together with learning in the broadest sense—formal and informal education, research and exploration—contributes to and enhances creativity. The greater our all-encompassing collection of experiences and knowledge becomes, the better able we are to make connections and apply creativity to problem-solving situations. As a result, the learning process should be continual. It is not a segregated activity, conducted for certain hours, in certain places, and at certain times.

Prior to understanding the creative process, it is important to make a couple of distinctions. First, for one to become creative, he or she must surrender their intellect to intuition: a direct knowing without conscious reasoning. Intuition has always been a powerful mainstay of problem solving, but it has been denied as a tool in the era of overdependence on analysis especially in business. Second, we must destroy judgements and create curiosity. If we are concerned with judgement either self or from others, we cannot possibly hope to develop fresh ideas if we are afraid of risking failure. Try to  judge an idea too soon and you won't be able to see how it meets its potential.

Creative problem solving compared to non-creative problem solving requires this destruction of judgement and opening up to intuition. In reality, true creativity seems full of paradox. It

simultaneously involves intuition and analysis, order and disorder, judgement and nonjudgement, fullness and emptiness, thinking and nonthinking (Ray & Myers, 1986). We must completely open up to the things around us and look at things in an entirely new way.

Gaining Control.

To facilitate this "opening up", a sense of being in control, at least of oneself, is essential to a healthy and productive outlook. In his book, *Gaining Control*, Robert Bennett (1987) states, "Out in front of every person in the world is a large window through which he or she views everything that goes on. Although it is invisible to the naked eye, it is very real. Not only do we see the world through it (looking out), but we also use it as a filter through which all of the

world's data is passed (coming in). If there is data that we do not wish to receive, we use our window as a shield to keep it away from us." It is critical to understand that we must have not only an awareness of this window, but control of it. Shielding ourselves too heavily from the "outside" will serve to hinder our creativity. The belief window is neither "good" nor "bad"—it merely exists. The more able you are to see what has been placed on your belief window, the more able you can predict future behavior and responses, explain past behavior and actions, and instigate needed solutions to problems

n o t e s

because human beings, either acting individually or in groups, cannot behave in a way that is inconsistent with their belief windows. While we may place our principles on our windows one at a time, they function as a group and are always influenced by the relationship they bear on one another. Therefore, the view through our windows is always a mixture of truth and misconception, and our decisions are influenced by the varying contexts in which we make them. "As a result, we will inevitably end up with some "principles" that are right, some that are wrong, and some that are shades in between" (Bennett, 1987).

Draw Picture

Paradigms.

From a creative or problem-solving standpoint, if we accept the possibility that some of our principles might prove to be wrong, we greatly increase our chances of eventually being right. For example, Thomas Edison once said to someone who complained about his lack of progress in his effort to find a filament for the electric light bulb, "No, I'm making a lot of progress. I have discovered hundreds of things that won't work." By accepting the possibility that some of the principles and concepts he was researching might prove to be wrong, Edison greatly increased his chances of eventually finding an effective solution to his problem.

notes

When a glue that was developed by the 3M Company did not meet 3M requirements for adhesion, it was nearly discarded until someone found a use for it and created Post-it™ notes. Tom Monaghan, the primary owner of Domino's™ Pizza, watched his first pizza parlor go out of business. These examples illustrate the need for gaining control and understanding what principles we hold to be true which will assist in one's ability to take risk as he or she perceives it.

Joel Barker, in his work *Discovering the Future*, has defined one's way of looking at something as a *paradigm*. He defines a paradigm as a model or pattern based on a set of rules that defines the boundaries and specifies how to be successful at and within these boundaries.

"Pair-a-Dimes"

When one moves from seeing something one way to another it is known as a *paradigm shift*. When someone was able to look beyond 3M's adhesive "rules" to see a break-through (and very profitable) product, a paradigm shift occurred. If no one at 3M had seen a use for it, and hence, discarded the glue as being a failure, *paradigm paralysis* would have occurred.

Paradigm paralysis occurs when someone or some organization is frozen in the mindset that an idea that was successful in the past will continue to be successful in the future. For example, Albert Einstein suffered from paradigm paralysis in 1932 when he balked at ideas of nuclear energy—"There is not the slightest indication that nuclear energy will ever be obtainable. It would mean that the atom would have to be shattered at will."

One of Barker's best examples of paradigm paralysis occurred when the Swiss, who have always had a very respected history of fine mechanical watch making, discarded their invention of the digital quartz watch because it did not have a main spring and it did not tick. Therefore, no one would buy it. They were so confident the new technology would fail, they did not even protect the concept with a patent. Consequently, Seiko of Japan and Texas Instruments of the United States capitalized on the idea and turned it into a huge success. This, in turn, had the effect of diminishing the world market share in watches of the Swiss from approximately 80% in 1968 to less than 10% today. Also, the employment of the Swiss watch industry dropped from 65,000 to about 15,000 employees in a period of a little over three years. One can easily see the disastrous effects of paradigm paralysis.

Frame of Mind.

When approaching a problem situation, one must be in the right frame of mind. Therefore, to foster effective creativity in the problem-solving process, one should develop the following mental characteristics:

- ATTITUDE—One must truly believe that the problem can be solved. The concept of logic cannot always be the driving force behind this. Often, logic has little to do with being creative. For example, Alexander Graham Bell wanted to talk through a wire. Another example: One day Bill

notes

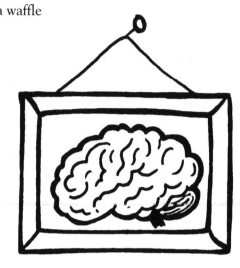

Frame of Mind

Bowerman was eating a waffle for breakfast that his wife had fixed him. While staring at it, something clicked in his mind. He took the waffle iron into the garage and destroyed it while making prototypes. What came from this and the pattern in the waffle iron was an excellent running shoe—the NIKE. Again, one must surrender intellect to intuition when making creative connections.

- **INTENSITY**—One must never jump to conclusions. The problem should be written and read several times. It should be redescribed in as many ways as possible combined with an enduring question and answer process. The problem solver should create a mental picture and draw as many visual images as needed.

- **ACCURACY**—One should always be in the mode of checking and rechecking solutions. Be proactive and never be content. Break the problem into smaller pieces and keep good track of a solution's progress. Do not guess as to a solution's probability of success. The importance of accuracy

"There is no use trying," said Alice. *"One can't believe impossible things."* *"I daresay you haven't much practice,"* said the Queen. *"When I was your age, I always did it for half-an-hour a day. Why, sometimes I've believed as many as six impossible things before breakfast."* - Lewis Carroll, *"Through the Looking Glass"*

can be illustrated by the following examples of being 99.9% accurate:

- 107 incorrect medical procedures will be performed each day.

- 20,000 incorrect drug prescriptions will be written over the course of the year.

- 18, 322 pieces of mail will be mishandled each hour.

- 1,314 telephone calls will be misdirected by various telecommunications services every minute.

- 22,000 checks will be deducted from the wrong bank accounts each hour (Working Communicator, 1992).

Although this may not be directly related to individual problem solving, it does illustrate the need for accuracy, individual or otherwise.

- **PERSISTENCE**—Sometimes, truly creative people and their ideas can take considerable time and determination to nurture and perfect. For example, twenty-one major corporations turned down Chester Carlson's idea of

Draw Picture

xerography. Dr. Seuss's first children's book was rejected by twenty-eight publishers. The ball point pen took seven years to invent and perfect. Instant coffee required twenty-two

n o t e s

years of planning. The zipper took thirty years to refine. No one ever said creative problem solving was easy, but the truly creative person has the persistence to see an idea through. World-renown management consultant Peter Drucker once said that, "the biggest risk is to take no risks." If one was to study the great inventors of our time, two key personality traits stand out: a fierce independence which creates courage and self-confidence to challenge the status quo and persistence in light of failure. In our current society, we focus so heavily on successes, our view is biased towards them. Therefore, who wants to read about failures? In reality, however, we learn far more from failures than from successes. Creativity is about failing and one's persistence to overcome it. To once again use Thomas Edison as an example, he and his team had to test over 60,000 substances before the successful invention of the alkaline battery.

- **PROACTIVE**—When one is continually in the problem-solving mode, he or she is typically involved in reactive thinking. The truly creative problem solver is involved in proactive thinking continually looking for alternatives, no matter how satisfactory the present situation might be. Change has been said to be the only constant in life. Therefore, one sometimes needs to challenge something that seems fine, because the long-term perspective suggests that change will be inevitable. Consider the frog. If you place a frog in a pot of boiling water, it will immediately jump out. However, if you place a frog in a pot of cool water and gradually bring the water to a boil, the frog will cook.

"Creativity is piercing the mundane to find the marvelous."
- Bill Moyers

Questions for Discussion.

1. List some of the characteristics of a self-actualizing person that you feel apply to you. Discuss why you feel these apply to you and why you feel the others do not? _____

_____

_____

_____

_____

_____

_____

_____

_____

_____

2. List some principles you might find on your belief window. How do you think they got there? What would you like to see there? What would you not like to see there? Cite reasons for your beliefs.

_____

_____

_____

_____

_____

_____

_____

_____

_____

_____

_____

3. Define paradigms. Discuss a paradigm shift which occurred in your life recently. Do you know of any ways in which you have been suffering from paradigm paralysis? _____

_____

_____

_____

_____

_____

_____

_____

_____

_____

Exercises.

 2A   Divide a square into four equal parts. Come up with as many possibilities as you can.

 2B   Design and develop your own personal "Logo" which represents how you perceive yourself.

 2C   Count the total number of squares in the box below:

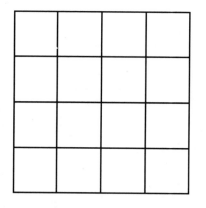

Exercises.

Journal. Continue to keep a journal of your ideas, feelings, thoughts, dreams, occurrences, how you felt about this chapter, or just about anything else for that matter.

Creative Process

Creative Process.

Some degree of creativity occurs whenever a person solves a problem for which he or she had no previously learned or practiced solution. Some solutions like this require only tiny creative leaps while others call for genuine breakthroughs in thinking. All of them require that the individual go beyond where they have ever gone before (Torrance and Goff, 1989). Regardless of the problem's "size," a sincere, yet concerted effort must be initiated on the part of the problem solver to achieve some desired result.

The Process.

The creative, problem-solving process, although intertwining and spontaneous, can be broken down into the following:

1) **It starts with some problem or need.** It is imperative that the problem or need be properly defined. If you start in the wrong place you can hardly hope to end in the right place. Once the problem or need has been specifically defined, the remainder of the creative process moves in various ways through the steps below.

2) **Information gathering.** You must have all the necessary and relevant information to effectively solve the problem (i.e. time constraints, available resources, what people will be affected, etc.).

3) **Digestion of the material.** An understanding of the material is critical prior to solving anything. A positive attitude is also critical at this point to enhance your emotions and frame of mind (see Chapter 2).

4) **Incubation.** You must forget about the problem or need and allow the material time to simmer so as to develop some flavor (if time allows) in your subconscious.

5) Sudden inspiration. This occurs at different times when the conditions become right. A number of alternatives will be created. Determining the consequences as well as the strengths and weaknesses of each alternative is important as each alternative may create new problems.

6) Implementation. You must take action and put all of your energies into the most effective and efficient alternative. Often, it is easy to allow procrastination, mental laziness, or just plain uncertainty to undermine your ability to act. Also, once put into motion, the chosen alternative must be evaluated and controlled to be certain of its success.

Another creative or problem-solving process proposed by Graham Wallace in 1926 consists of:

1) Preparation Phase. A problem is formulated. The problem solver attempts to solve the problem by brute force. Problems sometime seem insurmountable.

2) Incubation Phase. Unconscious germination occurs. Problem is allowed to simmer for awhile and focus is shifted to something else.

3) Illumination Phase. Insight is achieved. The breakthrough idea seems to come out of nowhere while the problem solver is engaged in some unrelated activity.

4) Verification Phase. Solution is tested. The consequences of the new idea are worked out.

Each of the above methods are generic in nature. In reality, the process is distinctive for each person and each idea. However, regardless of which method one decides to discuss, each begins exactly the same with the proper identification and formulation of the problem to be solved.

Problem Defined.

John Dewey, the great educational theorist, suggested that "A problem properly defined is half solved." However, the problem may not become completely defined until the **Verification** or last phase of the process. Many times, as the problem solver works through the process, the solution presents itself before the problem has been formally redefined. The solution carries within itself the redefined problem. Grossman and Wiseman (1993) suggest the following set of questions for beginning the problem definition stage:

A. A brief description of the problem situation causing you concern (3-5 points are usually sufficient).

B. What seem to be the major blocks or obstacles to success?

C. What does the problem solver stand to lose if the problem is not resolved?

D. What does the problem solver stand to lose if the problem is resolved? Gain?

E. A summary statement from A-D questions describing something that needs to be changed, starting with, "In what ways might I..." or "How to..." problem statements.

Einstein once said that the development of a problem is often more important than its solution which may be merely a matter of executional skill. However true this concept may appear to be, *finding* the underlying problem is often very difficult and often more difficult than solving it once found. Many problem solvers have a tendency to solve "symptoms" of the problem and not the underlying problem

"A problem properly defined is half solved."
- John Dewey

itself. While some problems literally smack you in the face, most do not.

Therefore, how you approach the problem is critical in finding and understanding it. Often, a good approach to get to the underlying problem is to use the "Why?" question and apply it to your problem-solving process. The purpose of this strategy is not to arrive at a correct explanation, nor to defend a point, but to explore it. This is similar to a child who repeatedly asks "why" in response to a long-accepted but unexamined explanation for something. With each proposed problem, ask yourself "why" it is occurring. When you arrive at an answer (a solution), ask yourself "why" again. If you can create a new answer (solution), then the first problem was not really a problem but in fact a symptom. Repeat this until you can proceed no further.

For example, a patient of a chiropractor came in to his office complaining of headaches. In applying the "why" question to the headaches, it was found that the headaches were not a problem but a symptom of a shifted spinal column which was pinching some nerves. In applying the "why" question again to the shifted spinal column, it was found that it too was a symptom, this time of the unconscious adjustment in walking made by the patient to compensate for having

n o t e s

one leg slightly longer than the other. When the "why" question was applied once more, the chiropractor could only develop a response based on a physical state (one leg longer than the other) which is the underlying problem. When given some new shoes to compensate for the shortness in one leg, the headaches began to disappear. Had the chiropractor simply just treated the headaches, the underlying problem would still exist, and the headaches would eventually return.

Another example of getting to the essence of the problem occurred while a student and his professor were backpacking in Alaska and a grizzly bear started to chase them from a distance. They both started to run, but it was clear that the bear would eventually catch up to them. The student stopped, took off his backpack, got out his running shoes, and began to put them on. His professor said, "You can't outrun the bear, even in running shoes!" The student replied, "I don't need to outrun the bear; I only need to outrun you!" (Prof. John Falconer, University of Colorado)

Focused on the attempt to find the underlying problem, good problem solvers are not only able solve problems but are able to "sense" problems before they arise. Thus, by sensing the emerging

"The formulation of a problem is often more essential than its solution."
- Albert Einstein

problem, the problem solver is able to find the underlying problem sooner before it develops into something larger. As a result, experienced problem solvers within some given context have contingency plans in anticipation of problems they are likely to encounter.

Problem Types.

A problem can also be defined according to three basic, generally accepted types: Analytical, Judgmental, and Creative. *Analytical* problems are typically seen as having only one correct, factual answer. Problems of this nature may include: What are the chemical properties of this substance? What is the median income of a high school dropout? How many times does the moon orbit the earth in one year? However, in reality, even *analytical* problems and their solutions vary according to one's perception. For instance, if I

Draw Picture

were sitting in the living room and asked my wife, who was in the kitchen, "What time is it?" She may respond by saying, "Its 6:00," or "It's time for dinner," or "Ten minutes later than the last time you asked," or "The same time it is in there." Even mathematical problems, which most people perceive to have only one solution, can have many different solutions based on one's perception. For example, 1+1 in most cases would equal 2. But to a preacher who is involved in a very intimate marriage ceremony, 1+1 might equal 1. To a biologist who is raising rabbits, 1+1 might ultimately equal 634! The point is that there are *ALWAYS* multiple solutions to every problem.

The second type of problems, *judgmental*, usually call for some type of decision as to right or wrong, ethical or unethical, moral or immoral, or yes or no amongst varying alternatives. The word "should" is usually a key word found in this type of problem. For instance, such problems may include: "Should we paint the house green or brown?" "Should I take this gift even if it may be perceived as unethical?"

The third type of problems, *creative*, tend to have no one solution which is absolutely correct. This is the type of problem which is the focus of this book. These type of problems offer an infinite number of solutions which are based on the various types of connections that are made. "Right" solutions are only found insofar that the word "right" means workable or feasible. These type of problems represent the majority of all problems that we as humans will deal with throughout our lives. However, these are the type of problems which happen to be the ones that most people avoid like the plague!

S.W.O.T. and Facts.

Once the problem has been defined according to that which is currently known and accepted, a S.W.O.T. (strengths, weaknesses, opportunities, threats) analysis should be conducted to identify your personal strengths and weaknesses in solving the problem and what

> "Discovery consists of seeing what everybody has seen, and thinking what nobody has thought."
> - Albert Szent-Gyorgyi

opportunities and threats exist in the problem's environment. It is important to realize that strengths and weaknesses are *internal* to the problem itself and the problem solver, and that opportunities and threats are *external* and cannot be directly controlled. By conducting this analysis, insights into solving the problem may become apparent sooner thereby increasing your effectiveness in solving the problem. Also, the analysis may eliminate some potential solutions immediately which would increase your efficiency.

   Some creative theorists believe that fact finding should be postponed. Some people seem to create best at crisis moments when their normal or usual ways of thinking prove insufficient to produce desired and timely results.

Therefore, fact finding actually impedes breakthrough thinking, and may, in fact, stifle the imagination by reinforcing the present perceptual state. By laying out the facts, the problem solver becomes grounded in this state and the attitude shift essential to the generation of new ideas becomes more difficult if not impossible (Grossman and Wiseman, 1993).

   I must disagree with this assessment of information gathering. Although excessive fact finding can be counter productive, not doing so can result in developing a bunch of ideas that are not feasible which is a waste of valuable time. With good information, many of these "ideas" could be eliminated immediately, thereby increasing both effectiveness and efficiency in the problem-solving process.

The fact-finding process is not a one-time affair. The gathering of information should continue throughout the process which will continually serve to qualify new problems and solutions and establish the criteria under which the problem is to be solved. Without the decision criteria, there are no standards of judgement to be used when evaluating possible solutions.

Alternatives.

When creating alternative solutions to the problem, one of many methods may be applied. Chapter 4 discusses many of these methods and a number of exercises are provided in the Appendix to help develop these methods in your own problem-solving contexts. Many of these methods utilize lateral thinking because it multiplies possibilities, and encourages the problem solver to think of many alternatives (Rehner, 1994). Rehner also states that with lateral thinking, you can pursue an idea even if it seems silly, because it may lead you to an insight or to a way of restructuring a pattern. Lateral thinking may prevent us from being trapped in blind alleys, or ways of looking at a problem that lead us nowhere. Whenever a problem begins to seem insolvable, lateral thinking becomes a tool for escaping blind alleys and for approaching the problem in a fresh way.

Sometimes you can facilitate the active search for solutions if, after having thought about it, you set it aside, let it grow "cold," then come back to it. Why? For several reasons. For one, you'll be able to look at the problem somewhat, though not entirely, afresh—enough

"When inspiration does not come to me, I go halfway to meet it."
- Sigmund Freud

n o t e s

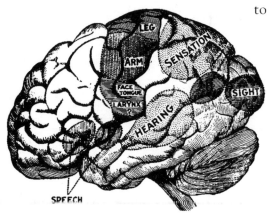

to note new things. For a second, this gives your subconscious time to process and organize what you have done and integrate it with your past knowledge to aid in making connections. For a third, studies have shown that the average mind can attend to only about seven or eight things at a time—that is what most of us can hold and process. After you stop concentrating on a problem, your subconscious mind takes over and continues the process of organizing the material, and if you have been looking for a solution, seeks to find it (Krathwohl, 1994).

Literature is filled with stories of individuals to whom the solution came "out of the blue" while they were gazing into a fire, sleeping or whatever. Edison and others have indicated that their best ideas came to them when they were in a state of musing—half asleep, half awake, just the state one frequently is in just before time to get up. Make use of your subconscious; it is one of the best tools a problem solver has (Krathwohl, 1994).

Creative problem solving by making new connections also does not have to produce the monumental, big idea as is so often the case in the American cultural system. The Japanese have been extremely successful making connections which produce on-going, incremental ideas which enhance current products, services, and anything else for that matter.

"The significant problems we face cannot be solved at the same level of thinking we were at when we created them."
- Albert Einstein

Decision.

Once a number of solutions to a problem have been developed, the solutions must be compared to the decision criteria to determine which solution, if any, is the most effective and efficient at solving the problem. If none of the solutions fit the criteria,

Draw Picture

then you either need to go back and develop more solutions, or your problem and/or decision criteria need to be redefined. You may be stuck in a blind alley, and as stated above, a lateral thought process can help you to escape it.

Implementation and Control.

After an effective and efficient solution to the problem has been created, it must be implemented properly. Often, many people feel so good about having developed a solution, they fail to properly implement it. Other times, fear of failure, procrastination, or just mental-laziness can keep one from properly implementing the solution. Implementation not only includes putting the solution into motion, but also evaluating and controlling it. In many cases, the solution, which appeared to be the best when implemented, does not actually solve the problem at all due to changes in the problem itself

notes

or in the environment. With proper evaluation and control, the problem solver can either make adjustments when needed or implement an entirely new solution.

The processes required for creative acts are the same as those required for all intelligent acts. What makes them more noticeable is how they are judged by peers, colleagues, or associates as being novel, valuable, or just plain interesting. Up to this point, we have primarily discussed only individual creativity and problem solving. However, throughout most of our lives, we will function in groups or teams whether it be at home, school, church, or work. Within these groups or teams, problems will exist which must be solved by the "collective," not just one individual.

Group Problem Solving.

Creativity in group problem solving can be one of the most important, and least understood, resources in organizational life. Effective and efficient problem solving in a group or team environment is not about <u>where</u> we solve the problem, it is about <u>how</u> we solve it. As a result, creativity in a team or group context is often diminished by:

- viewing it as an acquired skill rather than an innate ability;
- seeing it as "something other people do;"
- trying to move too quickly from creative ideas into evaluation and implementation; and
- concerning ourselves with negative outcomes rather than the positive potential of creative ideas.

Accordingly, group leaders should foster a creative climate which can result in a higher level of performance by individual team

notes

members. Team members should be open to each other's creative ideas, which ultimately will build a sense of teamwork. Often times, however, "idea killers" such as "It will be an awful lot of work," "Be realistic," "Stay on track," That's too weird," or "We've never done that here before," can find their way into the problem-solving session and quickly destroy the creative climate.

To avoid the possibility of such "idea killers" entering into the discussion, the group or team leader must nurture and protect the creative climate by teaching group members to:

- accept that creativity is not something they learn; it is something they have lost touch with and must "re-learn;"

- view creativity as a critical part of their roles on the team, regardless of their position or role;

- focus on generating ideas without judgement; analysis will come later;

- support and build upon each other's creative ideas at whatever stage these ideas may appear; and

- remember that being creative is a critical resource for affecting positive change in themselves, their groups, and whatever organization they may belong to.

Group dynamics are also important. A relationship amongst people in which mutual respect, understanding, and trust are present will assist the problem-solving process. Conversely, divisive relationships can sidetrack the process, regardless of how creative the individuals might be. The issues of the problem should be distinguished from those of the people. If they are not, it becomes very difficult to distinguish the two during the process, and hence, will aid in making for an unproductive session.

"Subconsciousness is the raw stuff of artistic, creative work."
- J. Castiello

Questions for Discussion.

1. Describe the problem-solving process and give an example of a problem which you solved in a similar manner. _____

_____

_____

_____

_____

_____

_____

_____

2. Pick an object around you and use the "why" question to determine its purpose and reason for existence. Then, pick some problem in your life and use the "why" question to get to the root cause of it. _____

_____

_____

_____

_____

_____

_____

_____

_____

_____

_____

3. In your own words, define each of the three "types" of problems (i.e. analytical, judgmental, and creative). In what ways are all three of these types of problems actually alike? _____

_____

_____

_____

_____

_____

_____

_____

_____

Exercises.

3A   A man has to take a wolf, a goat, and a large head of cabbage across a river. His rowboat has enough room for the man plus <u>either</u> the wolf <u>or</u> the goat <u>or</u> the cabbage. If he takes the cabbage with him, the wolf will eat the goat. If he takes the wolf, the goat will eat the cabbage. Only when the man is present are the goat and cabbage safe from their enemies. All the same, the man carries the wolf, goat, and cabbage across the river. How?

3B   Five apples are in a basket. How do you divide them among five girls so that each girl gets an apple, but one remains in the basket? (List as many possibilities as possible.)

3C   In a rectangular dance hall, how do you place ten chairs along the walls so that there are an equal number of chairs along each wall?

Exercises.

Journal. Continue to keep a journal of your ideas, feelings, thoughts, dreams, occurrences, how you felt about this chapter, or just about anything else for that matter.

Enhancing Creativity

Enhancing Creativity.

There are a number of methods and techniques to foster and teach creativity and idea generation, and although they vary, they all pursue the same end, helping people solve problems by viewing those problems in radically new ways (Wise, 1991). "There is no longer one way to approach a problem or situation. It requires a tool chest of ideas so that the proper tool can be applied at the proper time." (Solomon, 1990)

Some of these methods include:

- **BRAINSTORMING:** A group format, free association session.

- **BRAINWRITING:** A kind of individual brainstorming on paper.

- **SYNECTICS:** A forceful look at the origins of connections.

- **CREATIVE MANIPULATION:** The act of "reshaping" one's context.

- **FORCED RELATIONSHIPS:** The confrontation of ideas not usually linked.

- **MIND-MAPPING:** On a single sheet of paper of any size, the thinker draws a diagram capturing the flow of thoughts and attributes of something in a free association approach.

- **GUIDED FANTASIES:** The conjuring up of graphic stories or scenarios.

- **DREAM AWARENESS:** Conscious awareness of the subconscious expressed in metaphors.

- **METAPHORIC THINKING:** Seeing analogies where none have existed before. (Similar to Forced Relationships.)

- **ROLE PLAYING:** Projecting yourself into some other situation.

- **DISCOVERY THROUGH VERBALIZATION:** Free association with a tape recorder.

"What lies behind us and what lies before us are tiny matters compared to what lies within us."
- Oliver Wendell Holmes

Brainstorming.

Of these techniques, the most popular and perennial favorite is brainstorming. Developed by Alex Osborn in the 1930s, brainstorming is one of the oldest creativity techniques. It was developed as a way to get a group of minds focused on a single, specific problem in such a way as to generate a large number of ideas which could *later* be evaluated and judged. In his 1948 book, *Your Creative Power*, Osborn listed the following rules for brainstorming:

- Judgement is ruled out.
- "Wildness" is welcomed. (Free-wheeling and outrageous.)
- Quantity vs. quality is wanted. (Write down every idea as all ideas and people are valuable.)
- Combination and improvement of ideas are sought.

These same rules still guide brainstorming sessions today. In 1957 Osborn argued that creative problem solving (which he terms

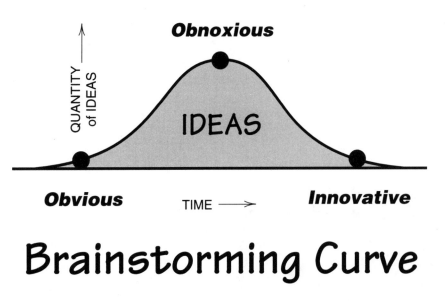

Brainstorming Curve

Figure 4A

notes

"ideational") operates differently from ordinary ("analytic") problem solving. Osborn felt that ideas which are generated later in the response sequence would be more creative. He therefore saw the process of creative problem solving as the unrestricted generation of ideas which are only subsequently judged as to quality. Hence, one would predict that instructions to produce as many alternatives as possible while reserving judgement should result in greater creativity (Buyer, 1988).

The brainstorming process, as shown in Figure 4A, usually begins with the most obvious and common ideas. During this phase, the individual or group is becoming comfortable with the process and is beginning to get the mental juices flowing. Once going, the process moves into phase two or the "obnoxious" phase. This is when people begin to loosen up and wildness takes over. This phase doesn't necessarily generate a lot of good ideas, but it does get peoples' minds working by making new connections while working off of others' ideas. Finally, the process moves into the innovative phase. During this phase, the energy of the process is still high, but the number of ideas begin to taper off to fewer, but more feasible alternatives. The truly creative and feasible solution usually, but not always, comes during this phase.

It is my belief that devoting a long period of time to phase one to allow people to get into the process is not an efficient use of time. Therefore, brainstorming group members should be given the problem prior to the process whenever possible so they don't come into the process "cold." This will allow group members to do some preliminary thinking prior to getting together which should reduce the amount of time necessary for phase one. This importance of time is detailed further in Chapter 8.

Brainstorming is a form of "Kaleidoscopic Thinking." When one looks into a kaleidoscope, you see a pattern. If the drum of the kaleidoscope is moved and manipulated, new, countless patterns are created (See Figure 4B). Each time a new piece of crystal is added to

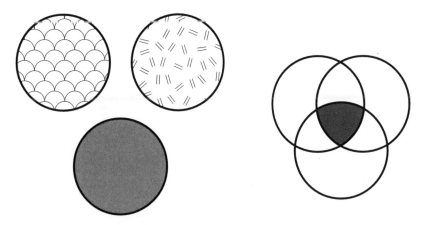

Kaleidoscopic Thinking

Figure 4B

the kaleidoscope, a slightly different pattern is created. If the drum of the kaleidoscope is moved and manipulated once again, a great number of new possible patterns are created (Parnes, 1993). Each member of a brainstorming group is like a kaleidoscope crystal who brings to the group a vast background of experiences, knowledge, and facts which no other group "crystal" possesses. When these "crystals" come together, an overwhelming number of new connections are created.

When leading a brainstorming session it is important to build energy and enthusiasm amongst group members while keeping the

n o t e s

attention off of yourself. Make the environment playful as this is more likely to create a greater number of unexpected connections. It is critical, however, to pay attention to your feelings, such as uneasiness concerning the direction of the group, and to be sensitive enough to read the emotional climate of the group. It may take courage on your part to explore with the group what is *not* being said. Also, the environment must be totally "free" from the fear of taking creative risk. In some cases, the status or power of certain group members can be a deterrent for some group members to take this risk.

For example, I was once involved in a "faculty" brainstorming session concerning policy at a small private college. As part of the group was the Academic Dean, a member of the "administration" of the school. While he was present, however, very few people ever spoke about what they were feeling. Very few new ideas were offered to the group. Since I knew from experience there was not lack of ideas in the room, the most likely cause for the silence was a fear on the part of the faculty having the "boss" present. After I had politely asked him to leave, an entirely new problem erupted—an excessive rush of talk in the room.

Brainstorm

> "Daring ideas are like chessman moved forward; they may be beaten, but they start a winning game"
> -unknown

Brainwriting.

Brainwriting, or the act of brainstorming on paper, is an individual idea generation technique. When one utilizes this technique, a list is generated of virtually anything that comes to his or her mind on the problem or subject at hand. The problem solver continually reads through this list with the hope that new ideas come to mind and that new connections can be made. The resulting thought is then added to the list. Brainwriting is a continuous building process which in essence forces the participant to utilize both sides of his or her brain to ultimately develop a wholistic approach to solving the problem.

Synectics.

Another creative problem-solving method is synectics. Unlike brainstorming and brainwriting, synectics does not strive for a quantity of ideas. Its goal is a sterner one—to produce a single, new viewpoint. Synectics was developed by Gordon and Poze in their book, *The New Art of the Possible*, which instructs readers in the explicit method for stimulating creative thinking about problems which are not solvable by traditional means. The sequence of synectics is as follows: First, one must identify the essence of a problem. Second, an analogy is picked that fits that essence. Finally, a kind of algebraic question is formed that applies the analogy to the problem. The desired result of this *metaphorical connection-making process* is a uniquely creative idea, not a list of alternatives. The purpose behind synectics is to teach a person to look at and understand connections both obvious or otherwise (Kawenski, 1991).

notes

"We are what we repeatedly do. Excellence, then, is not an act, but a habit." - Aristotle

For example, "What might have given a Scot the idea for a Kilt?" or "How is a rivet like peace?" Exercises such as these can help the problem solver speculate about the origins of certain concepts and/or objects which ultimately will develop a habit of thinking in metaphorical, connection-making terms.

Manipulation.

Grossman and Wiseman (1993) discuss another creative problem-solving method called creative manipulation. Creative manipulation is the act of reshaping the "what could be" to create a totally unique idea to solve a problem. In other words, reshaping the initially irrelevant to create relevance.

For example, a speaker comes into a room prepared to give a talk to a small group. The talk is scheduled to begin in about twenty minutes. She surveys the room for a lectern, but none is to be found. A search of all adjacent rooms also yields no lectern. She then asks the conference staff at the university about a lectern, but to no avail. Her talk fast approaching, she asks herself, "Why do I need a lectern? What would be the result if I solve my problem by finding one?" Her immediate answer is simple: she will have a place to hold her notes. She will be calmed by having something to hold during the speech; the audience can't see her hands shaking. Now she looks around the room again. She sees a wastebasket in the corner and in her mind's eye, turns it upside down. A holder for

notes

my notes, a makeshift lectern, "Aha", my problem is solved (the preceding anecdote is used as an exercise at the Creative Problem-Solving Institute in Buffalo, New York).

This is an example of creative manipulation. The wastebasket only becomes a relevant item *after* she had formed a future perspective in her imagination. Before making this discovery, she looked around the room without "seeing" the wastebasket. Her normal perception and arrangement of facts created a mental focus, or "functional fixedness," and when an answer was not apparent, a mental gap formed, which could only be filled by her creation of a specific futuristic vision (Grossman and Wiseman, 1993).

Forced Relationships.

Forced Relationships, or the act of Confrontation, is the ability to find common bonds between two or more previously unconnected ideas, concepts, or things in order to solve a problem. Regardless of the subject of creation, the process always seems to be the same (Grossman and Wiseman, 1993). For example, overnight shipping came from how the Federal Reserve clears checks, the idea of jet propulsion came from studying the functioning of a squid, and sonar from the bat. Regardless of the field—business, science, art, philosophy, music—the ability to force relationships is a key skill in creative problem solving resulting in major leaps from the juxtaposition of ideas or concepts which are not usually connected or linked.

When forcing relationships to solve a problem, one takes some seemingly unrelated real-world object or concept and places it on paper side by side with the problem to be solved. An exhaustive list of attributes is created under the "unrelated" object or concept. The problem solver then attempts to find some link or connection between each of the attributes and the problem to be solved and lists those below the problem statement. The items in this new list become the initial building blocks towards the solution of the problem.

The key to success in utilizing this technique is to be alert when making general observations. Be alert by looking for similarities, differences, as well as any unique and distinguishing features in what is being observed. The greater the number of relationships one can identify, the greater one's chances of making original connections. For example, a Shaker woman, Sister Tabatha Babbett, was working one day at a spinning wheel while she watched two men sawing wood with a straight bladed saw. By being observant to everything simultaneously, she was able to combine the two elements, the spinning wheel and saw blade, into a new tool: the circular saw blade.

A variation of this exercise is known as the Random Word Technique, which as its name implies, is the method of using some randomly selected word, often selected out of a dictionary or thesaurus, to generate solutions, ideas, or new perspectives towards solving some problem.

Mindmapping.

Mindmapping is a creative technique which starts from a key idea placed in the center of a page and branches out with subtopics through free association (See Figure 4C). If one tends to be right-brain dominate, they will find that a mindmapping format will help get to the essence of a topic, problem, or idea. First, the main topic is defined and focuses on main concepts and key words. Subpoints then

"When I heard the music it made pictures in my head . . . here are the pictures." - Walt Disney

n o t e s

Figure 4C - Mind Map

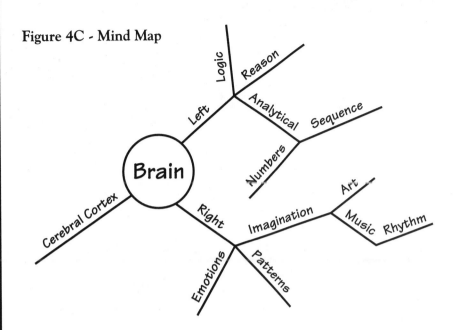

begin to branch off of the main concept, and the map grows as ideas are formed. Different-colored pens can be used along with symbols, illustrations, and pictures to aid in the process and make it more visual. Mindmapping creates a mental framework for breaking main topics into associated areas and subtopics. Although mindmapping presents possible solutions and ideas in a graphic and visual manner which tends to be a right-brained trait, it also logically organizes thoughts and ideas which is a left-brained trait. This creates a wholistic viewpoint which facilitates seeing the "big picture."

Guided Fantasies.

Through Guided Fantasies, one takes the problem to be solved or issue at hand and turns it into some graphic story or scenario. The story can be comprised of totally metaphorical representations, can be based on the actual meaning of objects, or can be a combination of both metaphorical and actual. Utilizing guided fantasies allows the brain to "daydream" so to speak and be as completely free as it would like. The key to using guided fantasies is to realize there are no rules, boundaries, or constraints. Everything and anything is open territory and free game. Evaluation of the story is accomplished at a later time after the mind has cleared. However, for this to be an effective tool, the story should be written down, verbally recorded, or visually acted out and recorded on videotape so it can be evaluated later for any possible solutions or insights.

Dream Awareness.

Becoming consciously aware of your dreams is another very powerful tool and source or genius for creative problem solving. Creative dreaming is the ability to transform one's subconscious thoughts, which typically occur in metaphors while sleeping (or sometimes while awake!), into a state of conscious awareness and understanding. This technique takes considerable practice and patience to develop, but once accomplished can prove to be a successful method to finding creative solutions to problems. For example, the idea for Dr. Jekyll and Mr. Hyde came to Robert Louis Stevenson in a dream, and the Periodic Table of Elements was seen in a dream by Russian chemist Mendeleyev.

Dr. Jekyll

In order to develop greater recall of dreams, one should begin by writing down everything, including each item, story, fragment, or bit of a dream, the moment he or she awakens.

> *"I have a dream..."*
> *- Dr. Martin Luther King*

60

Doing so on a regular basis will gradually increase the memory retention of dreams almost to the point of complete recall. As stated in Chapter 3, much of the truly creative development of solutions to problems is accomplished in the subconscious. An increased awareness of dreams becomes a direct pathway to that subconscious. The conscious process then becomes the manner by which the dreams, and hence metaphors, are interpreted since dream images can mean different things to different people.

Role Playing.

Role Playing is the act of projecting oneself into the role of something else, either another person, an animal, an inanimate object, a virus, or just about anything for that matter. This technique is very successful in helping to overcome bias and to look at all sides of a problem or issue.

Verbalization.

Discovery through Verbalization is similar to brainwriting except that it is free association through a tape recorder. With this technique, one talks for a period of time about everything and anything that comes to mind. Tell stories. Describe an object in the room and how you might improve it. Discuss how work might be different if you were in charge. The key is to just keep talking. Oftentimes, we as human beings say things that we have no recollection saying. In many cases, a creative solution will be "hidden" in this dialogue with yourself.

notes

"Whole"istic Thinking.

Many more creative problem-solving techniques exist. The point to realize is that whatever creativity technique is used, the desired result is to make new connections within some given context. This also requires the development of systems thinking. The truly creative person is concerned with how things work together and how one thing affects everything else. They look at the "whole" of the situation. I have entitled this method of thinking within the creative context, "Wholistic Thinking." An understanding of systems and how things work together not only forces the mind to see new connections, but also improves one's effectiveness and efficiency in all aspects of life. This includes anything and everything from understanding how all departments of a business truly work together to the teaching of students to look at how what they learn in one class is related to another to how one relates to their spouse and children.

Wholistic thinking goes beyond the "why" something happened and attempts to discover "how" it happened and what else it affected along the way. An analogy might be in medicine. When a medical doctor looks to fix a specific bodily problem, he or she cannot be solely concerned with the specific problem itself but also with how it is related to and affects the body as a whole. A wholistic thinker understands each and every aspect of the system and knows how its elements should be organized for maximum results as well as any residual byproducts and their effect as a result in the change in organization. They are able to project themselves to the end of the solution within its context. They are open-minded and conscious of

"It may be those who do most, dream most."
- S. Leacock

n o t e s

their own thought patterns. They are aware of their own personal biases and do not allow those biases to lead them into making unreasoned judgements by accepting certain assumptions as fact. They know a little bit about everything so as to understand. The greater the amount of information across various disciplines you have to work with, the more connections you have the potential of making. Knowing too much about a particular thing can overload the mind with specifics and reduce creativity.

Finally, a wholistic thinker is never finished. Problems are fluid. Each change or new idea results in a new problem and so on. The wholistic thinker realizes this and is able to adapt as situations change.

Creation is not making something out of nothing. It is organizing existing elements into new and different wholes to produce the desired results. However, ideas by themselves are utterly useless. The value comes when you apply them. It is the result an idea brings that makes it valuable. Peter Drucker once said, "Ideas are cheap and abundant; what is of value is the effective placement of those ideas into situations that develop into action." It is important to also note that an idea can only succeed when the self-interest of the creator and the self-interest of the user don't conflict. This goes back to proper definition of the original problem and to receiving proper feedback to keep the problem solver's focus on target. It takes creative effort to produce creative results.

Strategies to Encourage Creativity.

Sharon Ferrett (1994) provides the following strategies to encourage creativity:

❖ **USE CREATIVE GAMES, PUZZLES, AND HUMOR.** Turn problems into puzzles to be solved. Reframing a problem as a puzzle, a challenge, or a game instead of something difficult allows an open frame of mind and encourages your creative side to operate. Creative people know that they often get fresh ideas when they are having fun and performing an unrelated activity. When your defenses are down, your brain is relaxed, and your subconscious is alive, creative thoughts can flow.

❖ **CHALLENGE THE RULES.** Habit often restricts you from trying new approaches to problem solving. There is more than one solution and often more than one right answer. Develop the approach of listing many alternatives, choices, and solutions and imagine the likely consequences of each. Empty your mind of the "right" way of looking at a problem and strive to see situations in a new, fresh way. If you want to be creative, you must try new approaches, look at things in a new order, break the pattern, and challenge the rules.

❖ **CHANGE YOUR ROUTINE.** Go to work a different way. Order new foods. Read different kinds of books. Become

"...and the whole, though it be long, stands almost complete and finished in my mind, so that I can survey it, like a fine picture or a beautiful statue at a glance." - Mozart

notes

totally involved in a project. Stay in bed and read all day. Spend time with people who are very different from you. In other words, break away occasionally from your daily routine and take time every day to relax, daydream, putter, and renew your energy. Look at unexpected events as an opportunity to retreat from constant activity and hurried thoughts.

❖ **ALLOW FAILURE.** We learn early in school not to make mistakes and to avoid failure. Fear of failure undermines the creative process by making us play safe. Creative people know that if they don't fail occasionally, they are not risking. Mistakes are stepping stones to growth and creativity. When you take away the fear and shame of failure, you will learn to joyously admit mistakes. Also do not be afraid to look foolish occasionally. Creative people are not afraid to look foolish at times, to generate unusual ideas, and to be nonconformists. They tend not to take themselves too seriously. However, it takes courage to explore new ways of thinking, to risk looking different, foolish, impractical, and even wrong.

❖ **EXPECT TO BE CREATIVE.** If you think you are a noncreative person, you will act like one. Just look at the excuses you come up with for why you don't accomplish projects you say you want to. You have to be a creative person to make up such original and diverse justifications! Everyone is creative and inventive. See yourself as a creative person and take full responsibility for being an innovative and positive person. In other words, do not blame others for holding you back.

notes

SUPPORT, ACKNOWLEDGE, AND REWARD CREATIVITY.
Reward enthusiasm, new ideas, and creative approaches.
Plato's advice "What is honored in a country will be
cultivated there," is just as true today as it was over 2,000
years ago. If you honor new ideas, they will grow. Get
excited about new ideas and approaches and acknowledge
and reward yourself and others for creative ideas. Give
yourself many opportunities to get involved with projects
that stretch you and encourage you to explore and be
creative.

KEEP A JOURNAL.   A journal is a great way to catch the
beginnings of creative thought. Keep a journal of creative
ideas, dreams, and thoughts and make a commitment to
complete journal entries in this book. Explore the first
stirrings of a new idea and jot it down to develop and
explore later. Get to know your colorful, expressive, and
imaginative self. Write down dreams, draw pictures, and
include jokes and cartoons. A journal will help you shape
your thoughts and take action. Make time for writing, for
reflecting, and for recording creative hunches. Collect
stories of creative people. Write in your journal about the
risks you take and the ideas you have that are imaginative
and different (Ferrett, 1994).

*"Why is it I get my best
ideas in the morning while
I'm shaving?"*
- Albert Einstein

Questions for Discussion.

1. List and describe the problem-solving and creativity enhancing techniques as described in this chapter. Which of these processes do you like the best and why? _____

_____

_____

_____

_____

_____

_____

_____

_____

_____

2. In what ways have you used either the techniques detailed in this chapter or some form thereof in solving problems? What other types of techniques, if any, do you use or find that help you to be more creative? _____

_____

_____

_____

_____

_____

_____

_____

_____

_____

_____

3. In what ways can you challenge the rules, change your daily routine, allow failure, and expect to be creative in your life?_____

_____

_____

_____

_____

_____

_____

_____

_____

Exercises.

BRAINSTORMING EXERCISE—A soldier is found dead, face-down in the desert with a full canteen of water and a pack containing both provisions and food. However, he was not shot. How did this happen?

Solve the crime story below:

An elementary school teacher in Iowa had her purse stolen. The thief had to be Lillian, Judy, David, Theo, or Margaret.

When questioned, each child made three statements:

LILLIAN: (1) I didn't take the purse. (2) I have never in my life stolen anything. (3) Theo did it.

JUDY: (4) I didn't take the purse. (5) My daddy is rich enough, and I have a purse of my own. (6) Margaret knows who did it.

DAVID: (7) I didn't take the purse. (8) I didn't know Margaret before I enrolled in this school. (9) Theo did it.

THEO: (10) I am not guilty. (11) Margaret did it. (12) Lillian is lying when she says I stole the purse.

MARGARET: (13) I didn't take the teacher's purse. (14) Judy is guilty. (15) David can vouch for me because he has known me since I was born.

Later, each child admitted that two of his or her statements were true and one was false. Assuming this is true, who stole the purse?

Sketch a different tree as seen by each of the following: 1) Home Developer 2) Publisher 3) Architect 4) Lawyer 5) Psychologist 6) Designer

Exercises.

Journal. Continue to keep a journal of your ideas, feelings, thoughts, dreams, occurrences, how you felt about this chapter, or just about anything else for that matter.

5
Ask & Listen

Ask and Listen.

There are two very important requirements which are necessary for creative problem solving: Listening and the ability to ask good (sometimes "dumb") questions. By truly paying attention and listening effectively, one can be immersed into a new way of thinking about a problem, and its definition will become clear.

Questioning.

Implicitly or explicitly, creativity always begins with a question, and as a result, the quality of your creativity is determined by the quality of your questions—by the way you frame your approach to circumstances, problems, needs and opportunities. A creative approach makes life a questioning process as creative people are curious and interested in everything. Michael Ray and Rochelle Myers (1986) define a question as follows:

- ✔ A question is an opening to creation.
- ✔ A question is an unsettled and unsettling issue.
- ✔ A question is an invitation to creativity.
- ✔ A question is a beginning of adventure.
- ✔ A question is seductive foreplay.
- ✔ A question is a disguised answer.
- ✔ A question pokes and prods that which has not yet been poked and prodded.
- ✔ A question is a point of departure.
- ✔ A question has no end and no beginning.
- ✔ A question wants a playmate.

Whether a question is good or dumb is a matter of perception. "Dumb" questions can be born of observation, curiosity, rumination,

"The only dumb question is the one you don't ask."
- unknown

notes

aspiration, or acknowledged ignorance. A dumb question can be dumb in the same way a child is wise. Such questions have no expectations, assumptions, or illusions; they leap over hearsay and convoluted thinking to go straight to the heart of the issue (Ray & Myers, 1986). The ability to ask questions is one of the most important of all creative skills. Usually, finding the right solution to a problem may be as simple as asking the right question.

Listening.

Listening, not hearing, is a skill which is often forgotten in creativity training. This is unfortunate, because the most dynamic speech is a waste of time if it is not heard. Listening becomes critical during the initial problem identification and formulation stage discussed in Chapter 3. Problem finding becomes increasingly more difficult if you haven't "heard" the initial facts necessary to develop an understanding of the problem and its environment.

Most people tend to think of themselves as good listeners. However, research indicates that most people use less then 25 percent of their listening potential. Listening and hearing are not synonymous. One will always hear a message—unless he or she has some medical problem—but may not truly listen to its intent

and content. Listening is an intensive mental effort to be fully attentive and focused while observing and concentrating on the details. It requires energy and constant discipline. As Sharon Ferrett states, "Active listening means focusing on the whole message, observing body language, and seeking to understand the intent." (Ferrett, 1994)

Robert Kreitner (1986) discusses the listening process and gives some tips for more effective listening. "Listening takes place at two steps in the communications process. First, the receiver must listen in order to understand the original message. Then, the sender becomes a listener when attempting to understand subsequent feedback. Identical listening skills come into play at both ends.

We can hear and process information much more quickly than the normal speaker can talk. Consequently, listeners have some slack time, even though it may be only microseconds, during which they alternatively can daydream or analyze the information received and plan a response. Effective listeners know how to put that slack time to good use."

"Here are some practical tips for more effective listening:

✓ Tolerate silence. Listeners who rush to fill momentary silences cease being listeners.

✓ Ask stimulating open-ended questions, ones that require more than merely a yes or no answer.

✓ Encourage the speaker with attentive eye contact, alert posture, and verbal encouragers such as "um-hmm," "yes," and "I see." Occasionally repeating the speaker's last few words also helps.

✓ Paraphrase. Periodically restate in your own words what you

> "It is a luxury to be understood."
> - Ralph Waldo Emerson

have just heard.

✔ Reflect emotion and feelings to show that you are a sympathetic listener.

✔ Know your biases and prejudices and attempt to correct for them.

✔ Avoid premature judgements about what is being said.

✔ Summarize. Briefly highlight what the speaker has just finished saying to bring out possible misunderstandings."
(Kreitner, 1986)

Paying attention is a critical ingredient for active listening. If one is mentally preoccupied, this becomes a major barrier to effective listening. As a result, the listener must focus his or her attention, concentrate on the subject, keep a positive attitude, and have his or her mind in the present. The listener must be aware of his or her feelings, judgements, and thoughts and be able to let go of them while focusing on the message. Try to imagine a mental picture of what is being said. Listen with empathy and with the intention to understand. Active listening requires one to live totally in the moment.

Barriers.

As with most things dealing with the mind, there are barriers to creativity, otherwise known as "idea assassins." The biggest assassin is the little voice in one's head which continually tells he or she all the reasons why he or she cannot do something and all the reasons why something will not work. Most individuals believe his or her own perception to be the ultimate truth, even when the facts contradict it. Perception, therefore, becomes a self-fulfilling prophecy. Other assassins include a fear of failure, quick judgement, an emphasis on

logic, being too rational, having to have a right answer, having to follow the "perceived" rules, being practical (which implies being judgmental), stereotyping, limiting the problem unnecessarily, an avoidance of ambiguity, information overload, believing that to error is wrong, believing that playing is a waste of time and foolishness, and a preconceived area of expertise (expertitis). Another assassin is constipated thinking. This occurs when a person gets stuck in one particular focus of thought. The more focused he or she becomes, the less he or she is able to think of new ways to resolve the problem.

"Failure is not failure, but an opportunity to begin again, more intelligently."
- Henry Ford

Perceptions.

Often, we can listen to the same problem and yet have very different views. In fact, we often will perceive ourselves and the world around us in ways that reflect our individual values, experiences, knowledge, and personalities. We are also selective about what we perceive. This concept of varying perspectives—how we select, organize, and interpret the stimuli around us—is often explained by understanding that, as individuals, we each see the world through a different set of eyeglasses. To become an effective problem solver, it is critical to become aware of both your own set of eyeglasses and those of others (see also "Gaining Control" in Chapter 2.) As Jan Rehner states, "Exploring an issue from multiple perspectives means that you can multiply your opportunities to see more and to learn more from the views of others. Besides enriching your own perspective, this kind of active exploration can also minimize distortions in thinking caused by communication bias." (Rehner, 1994)

Therefore, we must not only learn to generate multiple perspectives and effectively "listen" to them, but also learn to shift our own patterns of thinking. There is enormous power in shifting your perception and gaining a new way of seeing things. This will aid in appreciating the complexities of a problem and increasing your understanding of it.

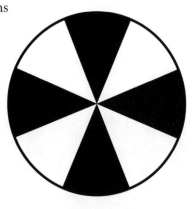

Figure 5A

Figure 5B

For example, in **FIGURE 5A**, depending on the shift of your focus, you either see four white triangles on a black background or visa versa. In **FIGURE 5B**, depending on the shift of your focus, you either see a goblet or two people facing one another. In **FIGURE 5C**, there are two figures, a young lady and an old woman. Can you shift your focus to see them both? In **FIGURE 5D**, the lines of the box are actually perfectly straight and at right angles to one another. In **FIGURE 5E**, Part A, the line segments between the two sets of arrows are equal in length, while the line segments between the two sets of arrows in

Figure 5C

"What concerns me is not the way things are, but rather the way people think things are."
- Epictetus, 1st Century

Part B are not, although they appear to be. Similarly in **FIGURE 5F**, Part A, the two intersecting line segments are equal in length, while the two intersecting line segments in Part B are not, although they appear to be

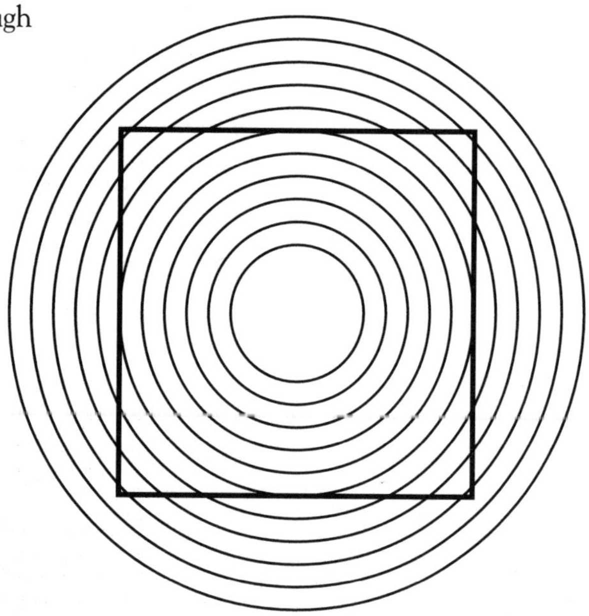

Figure 5D

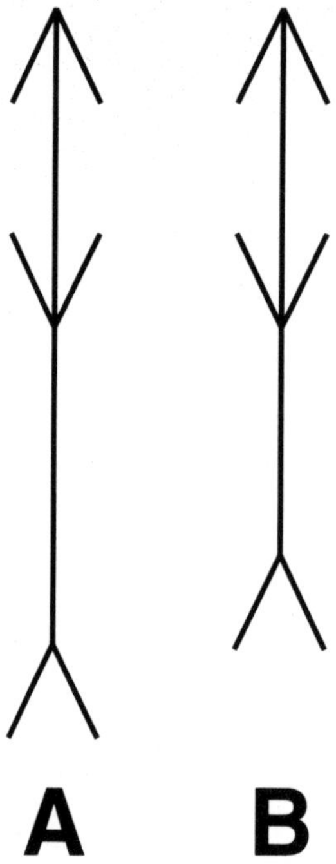

A   B

Figure 5E

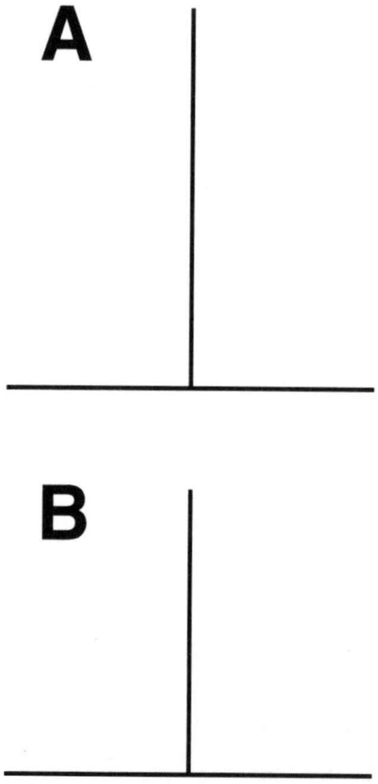

A

B

Figure 5F

notes

also. In **FIGURE 5G**, the white space between the black dots and the diameter of the black dots are the same. Finally, in **FIGURE 5H**, there appear to be shadows where the four corners of the black boxes come together, however, when you try to

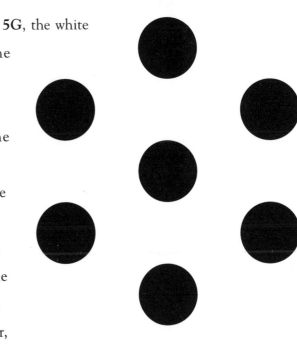

Figure 5G

Figure 5H

look at them, they disappear. We as people are conditioned to see certain things, depending upon our beliefs and attitudes. Rather than seeing "the facts," you see your interpretation of reality. This is called "perceptual distortion," which can strongly influence how you solve problems. To overcome perceptual distortion, you must make a concerted effort to see things objectively and openly, releasing yourself from your initial interpretation, judgements, and bias.

Draw Picture

Questions for Discussion.

1. Using the information in the text, what are some ways in which you can improve your listening skills that you are not doing now? _____

_____

_____

_____

_____

_____

_____

_____

_____

_____

2. Pick an object around you. Knowing that there are a number of different ways to view or perceive the object, shift your focus and describe it in at least three different ways. Hint: Role playing or changing your position might help. _____

_____

_____

_____

_____

_____

_____

_____

_____

_____

_____

_____

_____

_____

_____

_____

_____

_____

_____

_____

Exercises.

1) It is raining at midnight—will we have sunny weather in seventy-two hours?

2) A bus leaves New York City for Boston an noon. An hour later a cyclist leaves Boston for New York City moving, of course, slower than the bus. When the bus and cycle meet, which of the two will be further from New York City?

3) Which is worth more: a pound of $10 solid gold pieces or a half a pound of $20 solid gold pieces?

A detachment of soldiers must cross a river. The bridge has been washed-out, and the river is very deep. What do you do? Suddenly, the officer in charge spots two boys playing in a rowboat by the shore. The boat is so tiny, however, that it can only hold the two boys <u>or</u> just one soldier at one time. Still, all the soldiers succeed in crossing the river. How?

What do you see? List as many descriptions as possible.

Exercises.

Journal. Continue to keep a journal of your ideas, feelings, thoughts, dreams, occurrences, how you felt about this chapter, or just about anything else for that matter.

6
Vision & Goals

n o t e s

Vision & Goals.

One of the hardest things a person can do is to write out his or her goals and objectives, set priorities, establish action steps with due dates, and plan his or her course of action each day towards the accomplishment of some future vision. It not only takes time, but a considerable effort on your part to force yourself to determine what you value in life. This includes desired outcomes, what needs to be accomplished, how you are going to do it, and when you will do it. Chapters 6 through 8 in this book focus on the complete visionary process and why it is so critical in day-to-day problem solving. This chapter deals primarily with the goal-setting process itself followed by a discussion of planning and time management in chapters 7 and 8.

Creating a futuristic vision has become a motivation technique to improve employee performance and increase business productivity. It is my hypothesis that having a vision is also a motivation technique which will improve creativity and the problem-solving process.

Throughout life, we will be confronted by countless problems to solve and decisions to make. Some of these problems and decisions are critical while many are insignificant and fruitless. Some will require a rapid decision while others have no real time constraints. Some carry a high level of risk while others are risk-free. Some are complex while others are relatively simple and effortless. However, regardless of the problem or decision to make—its importance, complexity, scope, time constraints, and

> "If you give no thought to the future, you can have none" - Henry Ford, Sr.

n   o   t   e   s

risks—the only way to maintain a sense of focus as to what is truly important, and not just perceived as important, is to establish goals to achieve a vision. This allows the creative individual to be involved in self-enriching activities, to be flexible, to maintain a youthful spirit, and to *continuously* seek the achievement of new goals.

#1 Understanding Values.

First, goals must be value-based. Values are those principles and qualities that are of the highest priority in either your life or organization. They are the foundation of character and confidence. They are strongly held personal standards or convictions. They are beliefs about something very important to the individual or organization, such as dignity of work or honesty. Our values create within us a desire to behave consistently with them. For example, if an executive values honesty, the executive will establish a goal of trying to hire only honest employees (DuBrin, 1994).

Ralph Waldo Emerson once stated, "Nothing gives so much direction to a person's life as a sound set of principles." These values or principles are the basis for what governs our being, and when your behavior—what you do—is in line with your values, you will experience optimal control of the events within which you must make decisions and solve problems. Until you understand what you or your organization values, you will not value your time or do anything productive with it (Franklin, 1989).

Therefore, the first step to effective goal setting is developing an understanding of yours or your organization's governing values. Since we as human beings will not do, in the long term, things which we do not value as important, this step is critical prior to creating a vision.

#2 Create a Vision Statement.

From these values, you will develop a vision statement. A vision statement is not like a mission statement. A mission statement is what you are doing now, your current state of being, whereas a vision statement is how you see yourself or your organization at some point in the future. Once written, you will begin to develop and set goals, which will not only assist in your quest towards achieving that vision, but bring it into being.

A vision must be a means of self-fulfillment which is committed to direction, not success. A vision should also provide feedback. This way if you were to fall down, the feedback will assist you in getting back up to make another run towards the vision. A vision also gives priority to goals which you value, and when goals are valued together, you begin to prioritize them based on their importance. You can't do everything, but with a proper vision you can do anything. Setting goals without an understanding of yourself or your organization as well as the values and beliefs of you and your organization, is a state of wanting. Setting goals with an understanding of the above is a state of being (see description of a self-actualized person in Chapter 2).

#3 Setting Goals.

A goal is a planned-for-event. It is a visible target, something to aim at. It is a purpose. Goals give focus to life and your reason for "being." Without goals, you can strive so hard to reach the top of the ladder in your field or endeavor, only to find out your ladder was against the wrong wall. Goals keep you future oriented. Yesterday ended last night. Without goals, the future is that time when you will

"Give me a stock clerk with a goal and I will give you a man who will make history. Give me a man without a goal, and I will give you a stock clerk." - J.C. Penney

wish you had done what you are not doing now.

So, goals are necessary. Suppose the late Sam Walton had stated, "I just wanted to make a living, so I opened the first Walton's Five and Dime. Then, all of a sudden before I realized what had happened, I was the richest man in the country. Or Lee Iaccoca, upon reflecting back to his time at the Ford Motor Company, stated, "I just kept coming to work and they just kept promoting me until one day I was President of the company." Or Charles Limburgh stating that he was just flying around one day when he happened to find himself in Paris, France. This all sounds absurd, but no more absurd than you thinking you can accomplish anything of importance or significance without goals.

According to Zig Ziglar (1980), there are seven different types of goals: physical, financial, spiritual, career, family, mental, and social. Since most people spend a large percentage of their time in some organizational environment—be it corporate, educational, church-related, etc.—I would like to add organizational goals to this list. Regardless of the type, a goal gives you directional focus in whatever you are doing. It enables you to not only *solve the right problems*, but to solve them with a greater level of effectiveness and efficiency.

There are three classifications of goals: strategic, tactical, and transitory. Strategic goals are long-term in scope, usually five years and beyond. Tactical goals are intermediate-term in scope, one to

five years in duration. Transitory goals are short-term in scope, including goals for a single day, week, month, or even a year.

In 1953, Yale University conducted a survey of recent graduates. The survey showed that only three percent of the class had written goals, while the other ninety-seven percent had only a rough idea of what they wanted to accomplish or none at all. Twenty years later, the same group was surveyed again. It was found that in those twenty years, the three percent who had written goals accomplished more than the other ninety-seven percent combined. There are two facts about the future: You cannot control or predict the future, but you can control how you will respond and react to the future. With an understanding of your values, a properly written vision statement, and goals designed and set accordingly, how you will react and respond to problems will be not only consistent, but accomplished with a greater sense of focus and clarity.

Goals are multidimensional. Andrew Dubrin and R. Duane Ireland (1993) state that effective goals and objectives are:

✔ SPECIFIC.   They should be expressed in action terms, with clear directions about what is to be done. Present research illustrates that specific goals along with appropriate feedback facilitates creativity enhancement (Carson and Carson, 1992).

✔ MEASURABLE. Results to be achieved should be specified in

notes

measurable terms (preferably quantitative in nature). With measurable results, it is easy to determine whether or not a goal or objective has been reached (feedback).

✔ **ACHIEVABLE.** Goals and objectives should be realistic. It must be possible to achieve the goals and objectives as they are stated.

✔ **WRITTEN.** Each goal or objective should be committed to writing. Written objectives are valued more highly and are more likely to be achieved than those that are merely spoken.

✔ **COMPREHENSIVE.** Goals and objectives should be established for all major areas that play a role in the achievement of yours or your organization's vision.

✔ **COORDINATED.** Individual and group goals and objectives should be coordinated so they are consistent with and contribute to achievement of the goals and objectives of other individuals and groups necessary to achieve the vision.

✔ **PRIORITIZED.** To provide guidelines for the allocation of resources (time, money, etc.) and the resolution of conflicts, goals and objectives should be ranked in their order of importance.

✔ **TIME BOUND.** Target dates should be set for the achievement of all or part of each goal or objective (feedback).

✔ **FLEXIBLE.** Goals and objectives should be developed in a manner that allows modification if conditions change.

✔ **ACCEPTED.** Effective goals and objectives should be accepted by all involved parties. Otherwise, people will not develop the commitment required to pursue a goal or objective until it is accomplished (Dubrin and Ireland, 1993).

Goals represent a challenge—something to be reached for—and therefore provide a motivational aspect. People usually feel good about themselves and what they do when they have successfully achieved a challenging goal. Goals also create personal commitment towards achievement. Each time you achieve a long-term goal, it is the result of reaching many smaller, short-term goals which are a great source of motivation. Each time you achieve a short-term goal, you have in essence built greater confidence and motivation to strive towards the next goal.   However, with the achievement of every goal there is a sacrifice. You can never achieve a goal without it costing something. When Babe Ruth left the game of baseball, he set a record for the most home runs hit by a single player. He also had struck out more than any other player. Years later, Hank Aaron broke Babe Ruth's home run record. He was also near the top (and not by many) in strike outs. Properly set goals and objectives allow you to remain focused and overcome the numerous problems and short-range failures you will face along the way. However, remember that a failure is only a failure if you learn nothing from it and do not move on. A vision and properly set goals will help keep you focused and moving forward.

"Do not let the future be held hostage by the past" - Neal Maxwell

notes

In summary, an effective goal focuses primarily on results rather than activity. It identifies where you want to be, and, in the process, helps determine where you are. It gives you important information on how to get there, and it tells you when you have arrived. It unifies your efforts and energy. It gives meaning and purpose to all you do. And it can finally translate itself into daily activities such as problem solving so that you are proactive, you are in charge of your life, you are making happen each day the things that will enable you to fulfill your personal or organizational vision statement (Covey, 1989).

Draw Picture

Questions for Discussion.

1. After spending some time alone thinking about it, list those items which you value in your life with a qualifier statement for each. Be honest with yourself. When finished, go through and prioritize your values. Are you currently living according to your values? Why or why not?_____

_____

_____

_____

_____

_____

_____

_____

_____

_____

_____

_____

_____

_____

_____

_____

_____

2. Based on your values, write a comprehensive vision statement for your life. This can be as long as you would like, but it should also be specific. Are you currently on your way towards achieving this vision? If so, how? If not, what is holding you back?_____

_____

_____

_____

_____

_____

_____

_____

_____

_____

_____

_____

_____

_____

Exercises.

Develop the necessary strategic (5+ years) goals to achieve your vision as written on the preceding page.

Develop the necessary tactical (1-5 years) goals to achieve the strategic goals written above.

6C Develop the necessary transitory (less than 1 year) goals to achieve the tactical goals written above.

Exercises.

Journal. Continue to keep a journal of your ideas, feelings, thoughts, dreams, occurrences, how you felt about this chapter, or just about anything else for that matter.

7
Action Planning

Action Planning.

Planning is the development of a strategy or a course of action with the intent to achieve some goal or objective or solve a particular problem. It is nothing more than predetermining the course of events in your life or organization. However, it is the key to gaining control over the course of those events. Planning is a comprehensive process involving a series of overlapping and interrelated elements, or stages. Planning helps to reduce the risk in decision-making and problem solving. A plan offers a predetermined direction, while not having one causes confusion, uncertainty, and waste. It creates coordination and consistency in all problem solving and decision making.

As detailed in Chapter 6, prior to actual planning you must first become aware and understand your governing values. Then, you must create a comprehensive vision statement followed by the development of the necessary goals and objectives to achieve it. By doing so, you have a true target to aim at and something to strive for. Your goals and objectives become the focus of all your planning efforts. As stated in Chapter 6, your goals and objectives identify where you want to be, and, in the process, help determine where you are.

#4 Current Situation.

Therefore, the forth step in the visionary process is to define your present situation. Knowing the starting point (present situation) and ending point (vision and goals) is essential in developing an effective plan. For example, you were captured while serving in World War II by a radical faction of Hitler's SS. They blindfolded you and placed you in the trunk of a car which took you to a distant

remote island prison camp. You know once there your job is to escape since you are holding vital information for the allies. However, you have no idea where you are being held. Do you see the difficulty in developing an effective plan to accomplish this? Even if you know where you have to go, you still have a planning problem. It is just as critical in the planning process to know where you are now as well as where it is you are going. Establishing your current situation will also help to refine your goals and objectives.

To help define your present situation, a S.W.O.T. (strengths, weaknesses, opportunities, and threats) analysis similar to that described in Chapter 3 should be applied. Strengths and weaknesses are factors internal to you or your organization (capabilities) with which you have some control such as your attitude, work ethic, or accounting procedures, while opportunities and threats are external and provide very little control, if at all. The S.W.O.T. analysis will help you to anticipate any potential obstacles while planning.

#5 Action Planning.

Once you have an understanding of what you value, a futuristic

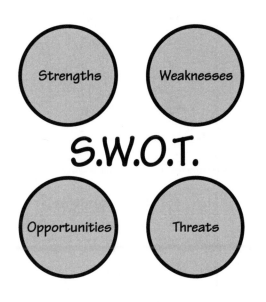

vision, goals and objectives based on those values necessary for the achievement of the vision, and an awareness of your current situation (start and finish lines), you now must develop an action plan for reaching each goal and objective. Developing the plan is one of the main avenues for utilizing your creativity and problem-solving skill as discussed throughout this book. The plan may simply be a solution to a short-term problem, a budget, or a master plan to reach a long-term goal or vision. Regardless of the scope of the plan, it must be *both* effective and efficient. There are many different plans which would be effective offering the same end result. However, one will be the most efficient utilizing the least amount of resources—time, money, equipment, etc. On the other hand, the most efficient plan may not be effective at all. Both elements are critical for success. The more time you spend on a plan, the less time it will take to complete it.

#6 Implementation.

Once developed, you must implement the plan for it to work. Although this seems obvious, many people, after having developed plans, abandon them in favor of business as usual, otherwise known as the comfort zone. To stay in our comfort zone requires no effort. It is

"What lies behind us and lies before us are small matters compared to what lies within us"
- Ralph Waldo Emerson

notes

easy, whereas leaving may require some pain and a perceived increase in risk. However, to reach any goal will usually require you to leave

Comfort Zone

your comfort zone. As James W. Newman states in his book entitled, *Release Your Brakes!*, "An adventure is the deliberate, volitional movement out of the comfort zone."

#7 Evaluation and Control.

The final step in planning is evaluation and control. Like with problem solving, planning does not end with implementation, because plans may not always proceed as conceived. The purpose of the control process is to measure progress toward goal attainment and take corrective action if too much deviation, both positive or negative, is detected. Through evaluation and feedback, plans can be fine tuned after they have been implemented.

Sometimes plans do not proceed at all as hoped. A contingency plan is a backup plan which can be used in this circumstance. Contingency plans are often developed from objectives in earlier steps in planning. The plans are triggered into action when you detect, through evaluation and feedback, sharp deviations from the objectives which cannot be corrected by modifying the existing plan (DuBrin, 1994).

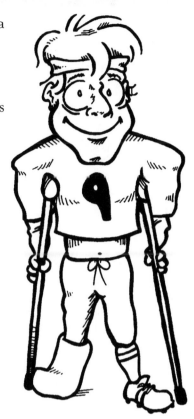

For example, a quarterback for a professional football team has the realistic goal, based on his talent, of making ten million dollars within his first five years of playing in the National Football League. He will then retire from football. To help ensure the achievement of this goal, he develops a contingency plan by purchasing a multimillion dollar insurance policy in the event he becomes injured and can no longer play.

Types of Plans.

There are three types of plans which are similar to the three types of goals: strategic (long-term), tactical (intermediate-term), and transitory (short-term). The three types of plans correspond with the three types of goals and must be coordinated as such beginning with strategic planning and working backwards. Strategic planning is the establishment of a long-term master plan based on your long-term goals and objectives to achieve your vision. All other types of goals and their respective plans for accomplishment must fit within the strategic plan. This plan dictates the strategy or comprehensive group of plans used to accomplish the vision. Therefore the strategic plan, like most all plans, must be value-based as discussed in Chapter 6.

For example, a high school student has the long-term (strategic)

"When you're receiving flak, you're probably over the target"
- George Hurley,
NIKE Inc.

Chapter 7   Action Planning.

goal of becoming a lawyer. Therefore, all of the student's intermediate-term (tactical) and short-term (transitory) goal setting and planning should be developed according to achieving this strategic goal. What law school to attend, where to obtain his or her bachelor's degree, what to major in, fees and expenses, school applications, required grade point averages, necessary curriculum and electives, extracurricular activities and organizations, and where to live are only some of the many problems to solve, and plans to develop required to achieve this strategic goal. Each has its own set of problems to solve, goals to set, plans to achieve, and time frame. As long as the student keeps focused on his or her long-term goal, all other aspects and situations of his or her life will revolve around and seek to achieve the long-term goal of becoming a lawyer. This is only a simple example. In reality, one may have a number of nonconflicting long-term goals which requires an even greater level of coordination in planning.

Since the planning process is very similar to the problem-solving process, the distinction is sometimes vague. On many occasions, the planning process and problem-solving process are one and the same. Sometimes, a plan must be developed in order to solve a problem. Other times, a plan will consist of a number of problems to solve. Whatever the circumstances, it is necessary to understand the importance and relevance of each in accomplishing your vision.

Questions for Discussion.

1. Complete a thorough and honest S.W.O.T. (strengths, weaknesses, opportunities, and threats) analysis of yourself to use in defining your current situation. Which part of the S.W.O.T. was the most difficult?_____

_____

_____

_____

_____

_____

_____

_____

_____

_____

_____

_____

_____

_____

_____

_____

_____

_____

_____

_____

_____

2. What do you consider to be your comfort zone. Please be honest and thorough in your answer. What will it take for you to leave this zone?_____

_____

_____

_____

_____

_____

_____

_____

_____

_____

_____

Exercises.

7A
Using the values, vision, and goals that you created in Chapter 6, develop a detailed action plan to get from where you are now (see above) to the achievement of your vision. Be complete and thorough. Also include what control mechanisms you will use as well as any contingency plans for any predicted problems or situations.

Exercises.

Journal. Continue to keep a journal of your ideas, feelings, thoughts, dreams, occurrences, how you felt about this chapter, or just about anything else for that matter.

8

Management of Time

Management of Time.

Finally, to achieve a vision the creative person is in touch with time and its importance. One secret to bringing creativity into your life is to truly to love what you are doing at every moment. As human beings, each of us has all of the time there is—24 hours per day, 168 hours per week, etc. We are all equal in terms of time which is only limited by the length of our lives. You must either use this time or lose it. Therefore, time must be managed properly. Time is a commodity. With so many tasks to accomplish and problems to solve in a limited amount

of time, we must allocate a specific amount of time to each so as to completely devote our creative energies to it.

Time Defined.

According to Webster's Dictionary, "Time is a continuum in which *events* succeed one another from past through present to future." According to the above definition, the basic element of time is an event. The key to managing time and gaining control of our lives is event control. When you say, "I don't have time," you are really stating that you have placed a greater importance or "value" on some other event. Consequently, the successful manager of time is

n o t e s

willing to do what the unsuccessful manager of time is not willing to do (Franklin, 1989).

"Valuecise" Tasks.

Therefore, within a given scope of time, it is imperative to rank tasks to accomplish and problems to solve by order of their importance. Importance is based on one's perception, however, and as a result, we will each have a different order based on each person's value structure. Since people tend to do first what they value the most, it is important that each of us determine what we value in life (see Chapter 6). According to the Franklin International Institute (1989), "Values are the base of your personal productivity pyramid. Next on the pyramid are your long-range goals, followed by intermediate goals and then daily tasks. Daily tasks are the means by which you can control the achievement of your long-range and intermediate goals."

Prioritizing is identifying the appropriate value and precedence of daily events. By prioritizing all of the various tasks and problems that require attention, you will be able to more

"A man who dares to waste one hour of time has not discovered the value of life" - Charles Darwin

efficiently and effectively solve problems and complete tasks more creatively on a day-to-day basis without spending precious time on nonproductive events.

Daily Task List.

A daily task list is a tool for controlling today's events so that you can achieve your goals. The following is a procedure for daily planning:

1) Select an environment free from distractions.

2) Review your values and goals.

3) Review today's prescheduled events and appointments.

4) Review the next few day's schedule to see what needs to be prepared.

5) Update your daily schedule from your monthly calendar.

6) Review your Master Task List (activities that need to be accomplished, but have no specific time requirements) for specific activities which can be added to today's Daily Task List.

7) Write the appropriate activities which must be completed in today's Daily Task List.

8) Review your prior day's Daily Task List for any incomplete activities.

9) Prioritize the activities (A, B, C) (Franklin, 1989).

When prioritizing, it is critical to assign to tasks a letter based on its importance. An "A" has a very high value and is assigned to vital tasks which must be done this day. A "B" has a medium value and is assigned to important tasks which should be done if possible. A "C" has a low value and is assigned to trivial tasks which could be

n o t e s

done if time allows. Some time management systems go so far as to assign a number to each letter thereby prioritizing the letters such as "A1", "B3", etc. Prioritizing forces you to stay focused on what it truly important. Many times, "C" items are simple, seductive, and want to steer you off course, but because you have prioritized, you will not be accomplishing them first due to their low priority.

Some people are natural prioritizers. They always seem to do things in a specific order for whatever reason. For example, when eating a piece of apple pie, what do you eat first and why? Many people answer the crust because they want to get the things they do not like out of the way first. However, will that get you to where you envision yourself going best? Some people are natural procrastinators. What do you put off and why? Is the task too big and overwhelming? Often, people procrastinate for fear of failure. In this country, we have been programmed that failure is bad. Failure is only bad when you do nothing about it. You must accept that failure occurs, and if used properly from a learning standpoint, it can be a stepping stone towards success.

Support Rather than Fight.

Although wholistic thinking, the simultaneous use of both sides of the brain, is the most effective method of creative problem solving, it may take time to fully develop this ability. Therefore, management of this time becomes even more critical.

notes

You will accomplish more in less time when you support rather than work against your natural mental preference. If you tend to be left-brain dominant, time management strategies like those just detailed will work best for you. You tend to be more organized, self-directed, and like to work step by step when completing your projects. If you have strong right-brain tendency, you may find that you tend to accomplish more when you focus on the "whole" picture rather than its individual parts. Hence, you may need more visual cues and greater flexibility in your schedule.

You will save time and increase your effectiveness and efficiency when you support your natural problem-solving style. For example, if you are primarily a visual problem solver, use lots of pictures, images, diagrams, and maybe even self-made videos. If you are primarily an auditory problem solver, tape your ideas, and play them back (see Chapter 4) (Ferrett, 1994).

Accountability for Time.

You must become accountable for your time. It is too precious, and too short. Be prepared for all the idle time that is part of every day—the 5 or 10 minutes of waiting for appointments, for the bus, or for dinner to finish cooking in the microwave. From a creativity and

> "I have a microwave fireplace. You can lay down in front of the fire all night in eight minutes."
> - Steven Wright

problem-solving standpoint, time is an investment. Michelangelo once said, "If people knew how hard I worked to get my mastery, it wouldn't seem so wonderful after all." We often believe in the "A-ha" factor of creativity where we will always be hit by some miraculous idea that will change the course of our lives and the world around us. However, as discussed in Chapter 2, some of the inventions that have tremendously affected our lives took many years to perfect. Thomas Edison once stated that, "Genius is one percent inspiration and ninety-nine percent perspiration."

Commitment.

Therefore, all of the time management strategies in the world will not make any difference unless you make a commitment to achieving results. Do not try to make too many changes at once or get discouraged if a time management technique does not work for you. Change certain aspects slowly until they fit your style. Be flexible. If it works, do it. If not, try something new.  Just make sure that you have given yourself at least 30 days of consistent effort in order to develop new habits. It often feels strange and uncomfortable when you leave your comfort zone and venture into something new. (Ferrett, 1994)

It's a paradox—It takes time to save time.

"The only limits are, as always, those of vision."
- James Broughton

Draw Picture

Questions for Discussion.

1. Define time according to the text. Does this definition have any "side effects?" How does this apply to your life in general? _____

_____

_____

_____

_____

_____

_____

_____

2. In the space below, create a list of things you enjoy doing and that you "value" as important (see Chapter 6 problems). Second, next to each item in the list place the amount of time in a given week you would like to spend doing each if you had it your way. Third, place next to each item the amount of time you actually spend doing each. Do you see any discrepancies? If so, why? _____

Exercises.

8A

In the space below, recall and list everything you did yesterday, for the whole 24 hours. Once you have written everything down, please indicate a priority for each item. It can be marked as an 'A', 'B', or 'C' priority. An 'A' indicates it is linked to a major goal or your top priorities. A 'B' indicates that it is something that should be done, but is not linked to an immediate goal and is not a top priority. A 'C' indicates that it is something that could be put off for a while or perhaps did not need to be done in the first place. When done, please add up the time spent on each priority.

Yesterday	*Time Spent*	*Priority*

Total time spent on 'A' priorities _____

Total time spent on 'B' priorities _____

Total time spent on 'C' priorities _____

Exercises.

8B   **Journal.** Continue to keep a journal of your ideas, feelings, thoughts, dreams, occurrences, how you felt about this chapter, or just about anything else for that matter.

DEFECTIVE

9

Quality of Solutions

Quality of Solutions.

In the first eight chapters of this book, the focus has been on enhancing one's creativity and its use in solving problems towards the achievement of some desired end, be it an objective, a goal, or a vision. In other words, the focus has been on the *creation* of solutions to problems. In contrast, this chapter focuses primarily on the *evaluation* of solutions in terms of their quality.

Quality Defined.

The word "quality" has become a common utterance in today's society. It is used repeatedly as an adjective to describe the relative nature of some product, service, or in this case, solution, in terms of its "value" versus something else in the same category. *Webster's New World Dictionary (Second College Edition)* defines quality as "that which makes something what it is; characteristic element; basic nature, kind; the degree of excellence of a thing; excellence, superiority." The American National Standards Institute (ANSI) and the American Society for Quality Control (ASQC) have defined quality as "the totality of features and characteristics of a product or service that bears on its ability to satisfy given needs." However, neither of these definitions creates any true understanding of quality in problem solving. In actuality, quality is a very ambiguous term that varies in meaning from person to person, and organization to

Degree of Quality

organization. Regardless of how difficult it may be, though, to generalize a definition of quality, people tend to have "feelings" about it and seem to know it when they see it.

Therefore, to define quality is to actually define a process; a process of evaluating the relative *value* of something as compared to another in the same category. This "value-sorting" process is the very essence of quality. It becomes a personal process whereby a comparison is made in the mind of the evaluator between the established, desired criteria (**Step 1** of the problem-solving process in Chapter 4 - *Define problem and establish criteria*) and what exists to fulfill these criteria (**Step 3** - *Creating a number of alternative solutions*). Criteria (e.g. timing issues, marketability requirements, and cost constraints) can be divided into two categories: **musts** (needs) and **wants**. The musts are necessary to achieve the desired level of "quality" in the solution and as such must be measurable. All potential possibilities have to meet the **musts** to even be considered. **Wants**, although not required, are desirable and are used to differentiate amongst the viable solutions that have met all of the musts.

For example, you are looking to buy a new automobile and your primary criteria (element of importance) is that the vehicle must be

Draw Picture

able to travel a great number of miles per dollar spent with little or no maintenance. As a result (based on cost-mileage comparisons), you will probably look at mid-sized, mid-priced vehicles such as the Ford Taurus and Honda Accord. At this point, all other vehicle classifications have been discarded from the possibilities pool (e.g. luxury, 4x4's, etc.). You will then look to your second criteria which is gas mileage and narrow the field even further. And so on until you have narrowed the field down to the single best automobile which meets all of your criteria in their order of importance.

From this perspective, you have identified the best quality vehicle based on your **perception** through a **value-sorting** process. If your top criteria were ruggedness, since you worked in construction, or luxury, from a social status level, you would have started the evaluation at a different point. For most, this not a very conscious procedure. It happens somewhat naturally and is based on judgement (bias), desire, feeling, and vision towards achieving something. Therefore, one must realize that each person's or organization's perception of value is different from all others as each has a different set of criteria.

Qualities vs Quality.

According to John Huntley (1986), it is also necessary to distinguish "qualities" from "quality." The first implies the separate elements, features, points of comparison, or component parts, some of which help to develop a quantified description. These quantifiable attributes of something create its primary qualities, such as size, shape, number, temperature, color, and weight. These qualities are specific to the object in question and set it apart from all others.

> "If a man can write a better book, preach a better sermon, or make a better mousetrap than his neighbor, though he builds his house in the woods, the world will make a beaten path to his door."
> - Ralph Waldo Emerson

On the other hand, secondary qualities, such as softness, roughness, goodness of fit, and taste, are not specific to either the object itself or its observer. These qualities come as a result of an interaction between the object, observer, and the environment surrounding them: "Do I *hate* this thing? Will it work for me? Does it help me achieve a goal?" The difference then, between primary and secondary qualities, is that the former is based on a sense of measurement and the latter is based on a sense of feeling.

It is this sense of feeling that creates the perception of QUALITY: a sense of "attractiveness," "excellence," "better than others," "worthiness"—attributes which are very difficult to observe, count, or quantify, but much easier to just have a gut feeling about. However, things (e.g. products, ideas, and solutions to problems) themselves are neutral and value-free. The value of something comes as a result of the desirability, purpose, and use that we as human-beings place on these things to satisfy perceived needs or wants and comes as a result of *choice*.

Values.

This sense of value was discussed in a slightly different context in Chapter 6. It was stated that an understanding of one's values was critical for long-term success in problem-solving

notes

"*Computer power is now 8,000 times less expensive than it was 30 years ago. If we had similar progress in automotive technology, today you could buy a Lexus for about $2. It would travel at the speed of sound, and go about 600 miles on a thimble of gas.*"
- *Randall Tobias (AT&T)*

and planning in the effort to achieve goals and hence, a vision. As human beings, we have a natural behavioral tendency to not do something in the long-term which we do not value. Of course in the short-term we will compromise our values, but eventually our behavior will shift back to what we truly value as important. Value is attached to something insofar as it is perceived to be an instrument for achieving some goal or objective. Therefore, the only way to successfully solve a problem with a *quality* solution is to understand or become aware of your sense of values as an individual. As a "wholistic" thinker (whole brain thinker) you will be better able to value-sort amongst the competing elements of the "whole," to compare, evaluate, and choose solutions critically for their total value. This will greatly enhance and facilitate the problem-solving process and ultimately the achievement of long-term goals and subsequently a vision.

Quality Built-In.

Consequently, as a long-term process, increased quality of solutions is a commitment that never ends, and therefore, it should be built into the problem-solving process. One method to build in quality is through an enhanced understanding of future direction. In Chapters 6 and 7, we discussed the concept of planning and created a model with the ultimate focus of achieving a vision. Through this planning process, a series of short- and intermediate-term goals were created with the intent of facilitating the progress towards some larger long-term goal or objective. These short- and intermediate-term goals become the concrete measures to provide benchmarks to gauge results towards those desired ends.

In the context of problem solving, the term "benchmarking" is defined as "a continuous, systematic process for evaluating the development, evaluation, selection, and implementation of solutions to problems towards the actualization of a vision."

The main advantage of functional benchmarking is the ability to create paradigm shifts, which often involve radical alterations in one's approach to problems. Functional benchmarking requires the ability of one to keep an open mind and develop effective listening and observation skills (See Chapter 5). As time progresses, you will have numerous assumptions challenged and will have to deal with an abundance of barriers. It also requires a sense of discipline. Of all the chief executive officers of major corporations in the United States, a large percentage have military experience. One point is clear: People who use the benchmarking process with a clear purpose or objective have a greater likelihood of achieving their vision than those who do not.

Value-Sorting.

Another method to build in quality is the conscious approach to value-sorting based on both effectiveness (doing it right) and efficiency (using the least amount of resources and having the least amount of waste). When evaluating the various solutions to a problem, you must distinguish between the good and bad based on your established criteria. This requires you to discriminate amongst the varying solutions to the problem. The easiest way is begin is by picking the extremes, the best of the group and the worst of the group, and placing them on the outer ends of the quality continuum (an abstract continuum that ranges from the "best" quality to the "worst" quality). Of the remaining solutions, pick the extremes again and place just inside those selected above on the continuum. Continue to do this until you reach a point where all of the remaining solutions seem about equal in terms of their "quality" or value level. These are placed at the center of the continuum. The result is a distribution of solutions from "good" to "bad" in terms of quality based on your perception and criteria.

Of the good (effective) solutions, which is the most efficient and what is the likelihood of its success? The solution on the outermost end on the good side of the continuum may or may not be

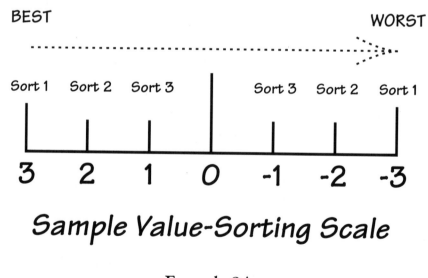

Sample Value-Sorting Scale

Example 9A

the best in actual terms. But at this point, it has the best "goodness of fit" with your values and established criteria. Once implemented, a close watch should be kept on its progress. If the solution is not achieving the required benchmarks or just is not working due to changes in the environment or your values, you should stop, reevaluate, and implement another of the good solutions or develop more solutions under the new changes and criteria. As shown above, both of these methods to build in quality should be used together to increase the overall quality level of your problem solving and decision making.

This approach works just as well with team problem solving as it does with individuals. In this case, the continuum will be broken down into regions and scaled with zero being at the center (See Example 9A). Once each team member has differentiated the quality and value of each solution based on his or her perception in the manner expressed above, the scores are tabulated. The highest score would indicate some group consensus. Although this is an overly simplified approach to the technique, it does demonstrate a concept of how to evaluate quality in a team or group environment. As Huntley (1986) states, "Whatever has value, must have value for somebody, but not necessarily for everyone. Nobody knows good and bad for sure, forever, or for everybody. Only time can prove the wisdom or folly of a choice." And with a strong vision based on one's values (or that of an organization) combined with proper planning and benchmarking, the "wisdom or folly of a choice" will become evident more rapidly and with greater assurance.

notes

Practice Kaizen.

Continuous improvement—the Japanese call it *kaizen* (pronounced ky'zen)—offers some of the best insurance for good problem solving. *Kaizen* is the relentless quest for a better way, for even higher quality solutions. Think of it as the daily pursuit of perfection. *Kaizen* keeps one reaching, stretching to outdo yesterday. Although the constant improvements may only come a little at a time, these small, incremental advances or gains will eventually add up to better quality in problem

solving. As Tom Peters once put it, "Good quality is a stupid idea. The only thing that counts is your quality getting better at a more rapid rate than your principal competitors. It's real simple. If we're not getting more, better, faster than they are getting more, better, faster, then we're getting less better or more worse." (Pritchett, 1994)

One method of practicing *kaizen* is not to get lazy about learning. In our fast-changing world, it doesn't take long for one's skills and knowledge to become outdated. Advances in technology

n o t e s

"Most of us will never do great things, but we can do small things in a great way." - Unknown

notes

and the resultant flood of information have made it hard to keep up. Although a college education is a good base, lifelong learning is the only way to remain a truly effective problem solver. As stated throughout this book, a diverse background and generalist thinking are critical for good problem solving.

Therefore, you must invest in your own growth, development, and self-renewal through regular studying, reading, workshops, seminars, college courses, and even yes, watching television (e.g. Discovery Channel, Learning Channel, etc.). Become a perpetual student. The more you know how to do and the better you do it, the more valuable you become, not only from an economic or social perspective, but also from a general problem solving standpoint.

Another method of practicing *kaizen* is an increased sense of personal accountability for one's problem solving and decision making. You must hold yourself personally accountable for the outcomes of your solutions. This requires you to think in very wholistic terms looking at the big picture and consequently, your own immediate behavior to see if what you are doing will bring about desired results. As emphasized throughout this text, you must continually shift from short-term to long-term thinking thereby delaying any short-term gratification for long-term successes. For this to work, it requires a high level of long-term commitment.

Ethics and Morality.

How do ethics fit in to the quality concept of problem solving? To begin, we must first discuss the concept of morality. Morality describes the social rules, norms, and standards that govern and limit our conduct, especially the ultimate rules of right and wrong

(Solomon, 1984). The key word in this definition is "social" which derives its basis from the word "society." Every problem is solved within the context of some society, be it the world, a country, a state, a city, a corporation, an organization, or one's own family.

Each of these "societies" has a different scope, and depending upon its context, can deviate dramatically from one another in terms of how moral principals are used to evaluate the adequacy of social policy. The members of a particular society will typically adhere to their system of moral rules, norms, and standards which will normally identify situations in which each person must restrain his or her self interest in order to preserve a system that is mutually advantageous to everyone within.

For example, when looking at the world as a whole, murder is generally seen as immoral. However, within the context of some countries or collectives of people such as a cannibalistic society on some remote island, murder is accepted as an appropriate function in life. The general sense of morality in Bettendorf, Iowa, could easily be seen as being very different than that of Las Vegas, Nevada. It is the majority viewpoint within these societies that constitutes its state of morality.

"Though I am not naturally honest, I am so sometimes by chance."
- William Shakespeare

n o t e s

The term *ethics*, on the other hand, also has many nuances. The Random House College Dictionary defines ethics as a "system of *moral* principles; the rules of conduct recognized in respect to a particular class of human actions or a particular group, culture, etc." Ethics has also been defined as "inquiry into the nature and grounds of *morality* where the term morality is taken to mean moral judgments, standards, and rules of conduct" (Taylor, 1975).

As seen, the concept of morality can be found in both of these definitions. Many philosophers and scholars, though, like to distinguish ethics from morality such that morality refers to human conduct and ethics refers to the study of that conduct. However, in everyday speech, we often interchange "ethical" and "moral" to describe good actions as we perceive them to be *right* within our societal context, and "unethical" and "immoral" to be what we consider to be *wrong*. Morality tends to have a religious connotation while ethics seems to have a secular connotation.

Ethics come into the problem-solving picture when the "accepted or defined rules" no longer serve to guide the problem solver who, as a result, must weigh individual values to reach a judgement in a situation which is somewhat different than he or she has experienced before. When greater emphasis is placed on one's system of values or sense of morality, ethics is being used in problem solving. In the context of the business world, for example, ethical considerations can be found in the following sample questions:

- Should manufacturers reveal all product defects?
- At what point does "acceptable exaggeration" in advertising become lying about a good or service?
- What rights do employees have on the job?

- When is the good of the employee greater than the good of the company?

The first step of the problem solver is to identify under which societal context the problem should be solved.

For example, in the 1970s, the Ford Motor Company introduced the Pinto. Shortly after its introduction, it was found that if a Pinto was hit in the rear hard enough by another vehicle, the car would explode. After some investigation, it was discovered that Ford knew of the defect before the car was first sold. Ford later recalled the cars so as to fix the problem, which was combined with a number of civil lawsuits. However, the total cost of not introducing the Pinto when they did would have been far greater than both the recall and lawsuits combined. *NOT* delaying the introduction of the Pinto actually saved the company millions of dollars.

Draw Picture

Following the public disclosure, many people felt that Ford had acted unethically in its decision to sell the Pinto. Were they unethical? It depends upon which society Ford management felt the most responsible to. Upper management is hired by the Board of Directors which are appointed by the corporation's stockholders. The primary mission of this management team was to "maximize shareholder wealth." If the management of Ford felt primarily

"Despite inflation, a penny is still sometimes a fair price for the thoughts of many people." - Unknown

130

responsible to its stockholders (society) rather than the public (society) as a whole, its lack of ethical behavior can be debated, especially when it required a hard accident to cause the problem in the first place.

You must also view the situation in terms of its time context. This was a period in which the Japanese were not yet big players in the automobile market, and quality as a whole was not the issue it is today. Although this is a highly abbreviated version of this case, you can see the dilemma. When solving problems, what societal context is the most important? There is no easy answer to this question, but it is one which must be established prior to solving any problems.

The purpose of this section is not to dictate what is ethical or moral in problem solving but to draw attention to it and how it will affect the "quality" of your problem solving. Consideration must be given to the societal context of the problem, who is affected, and what ethical issues exist prior to solving it. These considerations combined with an understanding of your individual values will form the basis for quality problem solving.

Questions for Discussion.

1. In the space below, write what the word "quality" means to **you** (not a textbook definition). _____

_____

_____

_____

_____

_____

_____

_____

_____

2. In the space below, write what the word "ethics" means to **you** (not a textbook definition). _____

_____

_____

_____

_____

_____

_____

_____

_____

_____

_____

3. What are some of the specific ethical situations you encounter and must work through from time to time? How do your responses to these situations affect the quality of your decision making or problem solving? _____

_____

_____

_____

_____

_____

_____

_____

_____

_____

_____

_____

_____

_____

Exercises.

You are alone and are out hiking one day in a forest. Suddenly, you come to a wide river of molasses with a very slow, but strong current. Somehow, you must cross the river, but there is no bridge. Please describe the situation as you perceive it including assumptions and constraints (e.g. the weather, time of day, description of forest, available natural materials, type of wildlife, etc.).

According to the situation in Problem 9A, create as many possible solutions as you can (no less than five) to cross the river which are based on your constraints and perception of the situation. Use the techniques detailed in Chapter 4 as a guide.

As described in the chapter, value-sort the solutions from Problem 9B on a quality continuum. Which are the best and why (based on both effectiveness and efficiency)?

Exercises.

9D

Journal. Continue to keep a journal of your ideas, feelings, thoughts, dreams, occurrences, how you felt about this chapter, or just about anything else for that matter.

_____
_____
_____
_____
_____
_____
_____
_____
_____
_____
_____
_____
_____
_____
_____
_____
_____
_____
_____
_____
_____
_____
_____
_____
_____
_____
_____
_____

Work

School

Home

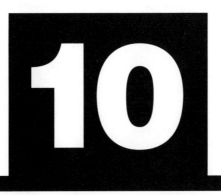

10

Creative Environment

Creative Environment.

Tony Buzan, the developer of mindmapping, states, "In the new forms of education, the previous emphasis must be reversed. Instead of first teaching the individual facts about other things, we must first teach him facts about himself—facts about how he can learn, think, recall, create, and solve problems." These traits can be taught and encouraged, but our current educational system is so overwhelmed with limited budgets and with socioeconomic problems such as drugs, dropouts, and teacher burnout, that not enough attention can be given to truly teaching students to think and be more creative.

Students are not being stimulated to find and define their own problems. Chaos is discouraged. Students are not taught to look for and value more than one answer to problems. There is too much emphasis on right answers and "safe" thinking (left brain traits) (Wycoff, 1991).

This type of thinking, which is encouraged by our various school systems—including primary, secondary, and post-secondary—is called convergent thinking (analytical reasoning measured by intelligence tests that tends to use rationality to move towards a single goal) (Harman & Rheingold, 1984).

Chapter 10   Creative Environment.

Much time in college classrooms is spent teaching facts which are soon forgotten after the final examination. Some facts become obsolete as newer measurements and techniques of inquiry are discovered. Much time and mental energy are therefore wasted in memorizing bits of factual information. What remains more or less permanently in the learner is his or her ability to think, solve problems, or create new ideas (Macaranas, 1982). Information and technical skills are imparted as ends-in-themselves rather than as ingredients in the process of human development (Litterst and Eyo, 1993).

Children, students, trainees, and people in general are naturally creative, unconventional, humorous, and are easily bored. However, our education system seems to encourage discipline, conformity, silence, and regurgitation of answers the teacher wants to hear, so these creative traits often become stifled.

Need for Divergent.

For an educational system to foster creativity, it must encourage divergent thinking on the part of the student—the process of thinking around a problem or generating different ways of looking at a situation (characterized by movement away from set patterns) (Harman & Rheingold, 1984). Currently, however, individualism of thought is discouraged in favor of the group concept thereby giving way to groupthink. The school system that wants order and discipline and the child who complies with the system in order to avoid failure and ridicule jointly establish an environment of mediocrity. The fear of failure begins to dominate the student's natural curiosity (Wycoff, 1991).

notes

> "It takes courage to be creative, just as soon as you have a new idea, you're in the minority of one" - E. Paul Torrance

The student is repressed by attempting to be "normal" and fitting in to their environment. "Our ambivalence about power also comes from lessons we learn in school. There we learn that life is a matter of individual effort, ability, and intellectual achievement. After all, in school, if you have mastered the intricacies of cost accounting, or calculus, or electrical engineering, and the people sitting on either side of you have not, their failure will not affect your performance. In the classroom setting, interdependence is minimized. It is you verses the material, and as long as you have mastered the material, you have achieved what is expected. Cooperation may even be considered cheating" (Pfeffer, 1992).

n o t e s

Group Concept.

However, in reality outside of the educational environment, group problem solving and team responsibility are not only very common but encouraged. If you know what your company is supposed to be doing and how to do it, and no one else does, very little will be accomplished. Countries such as Japan and Germany have made substantial economic and global leaps by fostering a team approach to education beginning at the primary level.

Creativity training will erase these negative problem-solving messages of our educational system and will allow people to get in touch with their originality, yet still teach them how to function as part of a group or team. The function of the creativity trainer, therefore, becomes a cooperative one where he or she will pierce the ideas of the students with probing questions to which they will have to find the answers themselves or as part of a group. This enables the student to enter into the spirit of inquiry which is imperative in creative problem solving.

Once people discover their creativity, they tend to be independent, self-confident, risk-taking, highly energetic, enthusiastic, spontaneous, adventurous, thorough, curious, humorous, playful, and childlike (Wycoff, 1991). While it is important to recognize the traits which encourage creativity, it is more important to remember that each of us is born with the ability to create. By understanding the process of creativity, we can enhance our creative abilities. By teaching students, employees, and people in general there is more than one possible solution to a problem, they will be encouraged to use their creativity to reach the most effective solution which is both novel and valued.

Transformation.

Much time and effort should be spent in transforming the ordinary learning environment, whether it be at a school, the office, or at home, into an appropriate environment which will not only facilitate the atmosphere in which the problem is set, but also elicit creative behavior from the student or trainee (Slabbert, 1994). Within this environment, mental games could be played with the same enthusiasm and competitive spirit as physical games to expose the student or trainee to the methods and skills of

Draw Picture

creative problem solving. Play stimulates the use of imagination which in turn facilitates creativity in problem solving. Through constant practice and exercise, the mind could be trained to reach its fullest creative potential. Practice makes permanence, not perfection. Finally, the student or trainee must be systematically provided with feedback as to the quality of their results. Feedback is critical for continual improvement and enhancement of what the student or trainee is learning and developing within.

SCANS.

The 1991 U.S. Department of Labor Secretary's Commission on Achieving Necessary Skills (SCANS) report entitled, "What Work Requires of Schools - A SCANS Report for America 2000," examined the demands of the workplace and whether our young people are capable of meeting those demands. Specifically, the Commission was directed to advise the Secretary of Labor on the level of skills required to enter employment.

The SCANS research verifies that what we call *workplace know-how* defines effective job performance today. This know-how has two elements: *competencies* and a *foundation*. The report identified five competencies and a three-part foundation of skills and personal qualities. One of the five competencies was an understanding of systems and complex interrelationships. The student would know how social, organizational, and technological systems work and how to operate effectively with them. They would be able to distinguish trends, predict impacts on systems' operations, diagnose systems' performance, and correct malfunctions. Finally, the student would be able to suggest modifications to existing systems and develop new or alternative systems to improve performance ("wholistic" thinking).

Of the three-part foundation of skills and personal qualities, one part is entirely devoted to thinking skills. The student would be able to think creatively, make decisions, solve problems, visualize, know how to learn, and reason. These traits combined with the systems approach are currently not typically being taught nor fostered in our general educational system. The government realizes that our students and future leaders are deficient in this area and are requesting that schools incorporate these aspects into their curriculums.

Our learning environment, both formally at schools and educational institutions and informally at the workplace and home, needs to be redesigned including its system, processes and curriculum. Not until creativity is actively applied to this environment will the process of learning become creative and instill creativity into the mind of the learner.

"Dive into the sea of thought and find there pearls beyond price."
- Abraham Ibn-Ezra

Questions for Discussion.

1. Describe some of the various environments in which you are a part. How is creativity in problem solving either stifled or encouraged? _____

_____

_____

_____

_____

_____

_____

_____

_____

2. You are the new superintendent for ALL schools in the United States with complete autonomy and control over how they function and operate. How would you change them so as to foster an environment of greater individual creativity and teamwork? _____

_____

_____

_____

_____

_____

_____

_____

_____

_____

_____

3. Think of an actual person or fictional character who lives in a very creative environment which appeals to you. Using this as a reference, how could you modify your current environment to become similar? _____

_____

_____

_____

_____

_____

_____

_____

_____

_____

Exercises.

Journal. Continue to keep a journal of your ideas, feelings, thoughts, dreams, occurrences, how you felt about this chapter, or just about anything else for that matter.

_____

_____

_____

_____

_____

_____

_____

_____

_____

_____

_____

_____

_____

_____

_____

_____

_____

_____

_____

_____

_____

_____

_____

_____

_____

_____

_____

_____

_____

Conclusion

Conclusion.

According to Angela Grupas (1990), ten percent of seven year-olds and some ninety percent of all five year-olds are creative. Between the ages of five to seven years of age we lose the bulk of our creativity, which is about forty percent. What happens at age five? We begin attending school where between 2000 to 2500 intelligence tests will be administered particularly during high school and college alone, asking us to give the "right answer." We learn to forget that many problems have multiple "right" answers (Grupas, 1990).

I recently read an article in *Time* magazine entitled, "*Are You Creative?*," which stated that research and tests show that by the age of forty, most adults are about two percent as creative as they were at the age of five. Although I have no way to evaluate these studies in terms of their research methodologies, I do believe in their accuracy. As I observe my young children in their endeavors, I am amazed at the connections they make to overcome a number of problems and obstacles. They have a tendency to be unobvious (in adult terms) and fresh. On the other hand, as I have viewed my college students over the years, I am amazed at how most have difficulty with solving the simplest of problems. When a solution finally was developed, it tended to be on the "noncreative" side with the responses being somewhat common in nature. Many times their solution was simply a slight rework of old ideas. I used to believe they just lacked the required technical skills, but in reality, it is their lack of creative-thinking skills that holds them back.

The creative process is never finished. As a result, this book is a work-in-progress. I will continue to research creativity in problem solving and its importance within the context of education and

training. My hope is to bring together teaching and learning as they now are perceived to be on opposite ends of the spectrum. The misconception of this separation makes it appear that teaching occurs at one end of the classroom, under the control of the instructor, and learning takes place at the opposite end, under the behest of the student. Teachers must be enlightened about the learning process and their role in it.

Appendix - Exercises

Another Counting Exercise.

Count how many triangles there are in the figure.

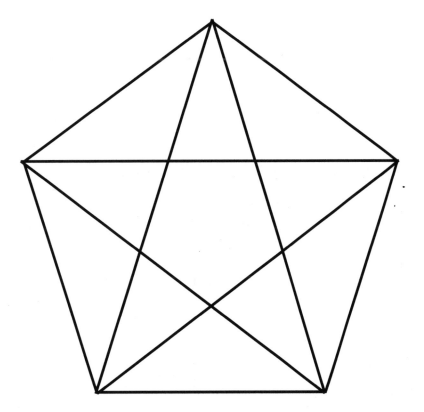

TOTAL: _____

2

EXERCISE

Superhero Group Exercise.

First, assign one member of the group as the role of the client or decision maker (this will be the only person other than the facilitator which does not get to be a superhero). The other members of the group will then select a superhero they want to be, either a "known" hero (e.g. Batman, Spiderman, Flash, Wonder Woman, Superman, etc.), or one which is created by the participant.

Each person will then be given an established amount of time (usually one-half hour) to create a costume out of everyday objects in the room. If this is preplanned, participants can bring premade costumes made out of everyday objects at home.

Once everyone is settled, the preestablished client asks the "League of Superheros" for solutions to some problem based on his or her persona character.

Created by Steve Grossman, Maple Shade, New Jersey.

3

EXERCISE

Worst Idea Exercise.

A) First, make a list of the worst business ideas you can think of (e.g. a solar-powered night light, a surf board shop in Antarctica, reversible diapers)

B) Then, take this list and turn it around to make each idea a viable concept for entrepreneurial ventures (e.g. reversible diapers—blue on one side and pink on the other)

This exercise can easily be adapted for a group brainstorming session.

Fogler and LeBlanc, 1995.

4

EXERCISE

Group Video Exercise.

Watch one-half of a movie with a group. Stop the movie. Each member of the group will "create" his or her own ending.

Watch the rest of the movie and discuss the results. Whose ending was better and why?

Fogler and LeBlanc, 1995.

5

EXERCISE

Group Picture Exercise.

A) First, have members in a group draw one-half of a picture.

B) Then, group members will exchange drawings which will be completed by the new group member.

When completed, have members discuss the results. Why did each finish the drawing as he or she did? Which "team" drawing is the best and why?

Group Comic Strip Exercise.

A) First, as a group, brainstorm an idea for a new comic strip including a frame-by-frame story line. Have at least the same number of frame captions as team members.

B) Then, have each team member illustrate at least one of the above frames based on its caption. When completed, place and tape all of the frames in sequence on the wall. Discuss.

EXERCISE 7

Group Theme Park Exercise.

A) First, as a group, brainstorm an idea for a new theme park including all rides and attractions. Have at least the same number of rides and attractions as team members.

B) Then, have each team member illustrate at least one of the above rides and attractions based on the "theme" of the park.

C) When completed, brainstorm once again as to the relative placement of all rides and attractions in the park. Place each one in its proper position relative to all others and tape in place. When finished, discuss the results.

8

EXERCISE

Group Communication Exercise.

A) Break the group down into subgroups of no fewer than two people in each group.

B) Then, have each group create a new language. The new language must have at least an introduction, descriptions for objects within the room, a positive comment, and a farewell. Each subgroup has thirty minutes to design and learn their new languages.

C) After this thirty-minute period, each subgroup member should pair off with someone from a different subgroup. They will have fifteen minutes to teach each other their new language. Once learned, members are only to use their new learned language and not speak in any other dialect.

D) Finally, have all group members place blindfolds on and reform into their original subgroups. They are to continue to use only their new language learned in Step C.

E) Discuss the results.

Kroehnert, 1991.

9

EXERCISE

Story Exercise.

A) First, assemble a group of miscellaneous objects within the room. The group should contain no fewer than ten objects.

B) Then, from this group of objects, create a story using all of the pieces. The pieces can be used as they really are or as metaphors representing something else. Write the story below.

Mindmapping Exercise.

As discussed in Chapter 4, create a Mindmap beginning with the word sports.

Sports

Additional Journal Pages.

Continue to keep a journal of your ideas, feelings, thoughts, dreams, occurrences, how you felt about these exercises or this book, or just about anything else for that matter.

Journal.

Journal.

Journal.

Workspace

Workspace.

This section provides extra workspace for exercises, note taking, spontaneous sketching, doodling, brainwriting, mindmapping, or for any other reason you deem necessary.

_____

_____

_____

_____

_____

_____

_____

_____

_____

_____

_____

Workspace.

Workspace.

Workspace.

Workspace.

Workspace.

Workspace.

Workspace.

Workspace.

Workspace.

Workspace.

Workspace.

References

References.

Barker, J.A., *Discovering the Future*. 2nd ed., ILI Press, St. Paul, MN, 1985.

Bennett, Robert F., *Gaining Control*. Franklin International Institute, Inc.: Salt Lake City, UT, 1987.

Buyer, Linda S., "Creative Problem Solving: A Comparison of Performance Under Different Instructions," *Journal of Creative Behavior*, Vol. 22, No. 1, pp. 55-61.

Buzan, Tony, *Use Both Sides of Your Brain*. E.P. Dutton, Inc.: New York, NY, 1974.

Carson, Paula Phillips, and Carson, Kerry D., "Managing Creativity Enhancement Through Goal-Setting and Feedback," *Journal of Creative Behavior*, Vol. 26, No. 1, pp. 36-45.

Cleese, J., "And Now for Something Completely Different," *Personnel*, Vol. 68, 1991, pp. 13-15.

Covey, Stephen R., *The 7 Habits of Highly Effective People*. Simon and Schuster: New York, NY, 1989.

De Bono, Edward, *Lateral Thinking*. Penguin Books: London, 1990.

DuBrin, Andrew J., *Essentials of Management*. South-Western Publishing Co.: Cincinnati, OH, 1994.

DuBrin, Andrew J., and Ireland, R. Duane, *Management and Organization*. South-Western Publishing Co.: Cincinnati, OH, 1993.

Falconer, Prof. John, University of Colorado, Boulder, CO 80302.

Ferrett, Sharon K., *Peak Performance*. Irwin Mirror Press: Burr Ridge, IL, 1994.

Folger, H. Scott, and LeBlanc, Steven E., *Strategies for Creative Problem Solving*. Prentice Hall PTR: Englewood Cliffs, NJ, 1995.

Franklin International Institute, Inc., *Time Management Seminar*. Salt Lake City, UT, 1989.

Grossman, Stephen R., and Wiseman, Edward E., "Seven Operating Principles for Enhanced Creative Problem Solving Training," *Journal of Creative Behavior*, Vol. 27, No. 1, pp. 1-17.

Grupas, Angela, "Creative Problem-Solving," *Paper Presented at the Annual Meeting of the Missouri Association of Community and Junior Colleges*, November 15-17, 1990, 13 pp.

Harman, Willis, and Rheingold, Howard, *Higher Creativity*. St. Martin's Press: New York, NY, 1984.

Herrmann, Ned, "The Creative Brain," *Journal of Creative Behavior*, Vol. 25, No. 4, pp. 275-295.

Huntley, John F., "The Judgment and Public Measure of Value in Academic Contexts," *Journal of General Education*, Vol. 37, No. 4, pp. 280-312.

Kawenski, Mary, "Encouraging Creativity in Design," *Journal of Creative Behavior*, Vol. 25, No. 3, pp. 263-266.

Krathwohl, David R., "Slice of Advice," *Educational Researcher*, Vol. 23, No. 1, pp. 29-32, 42.

Kreitner, Robert, *Management*. Houghton Mifflin Company: Boston, MA, 1986.

Kroehnert, Gary, *100 Training Games*. McGraw-Hill Book Company: Sydney, Australia, 1991.

Litterst, Judith K., and Eyo, Bassey A., "Developing Classroom Imagination: Shaping and Energizing a Suitable Climate for Growth, Discovery, and Vision," *Journal of Creative Behavior*, Vol. 27, No. 4, pp. 270-282.

Macaranas, Natividad, "A Creative Approach to Teaching," *Paper Presented at the Annual Meeting of the Rocky Mountain Psychological Association*, Albuquerque, NM, April 28-May 1, 1982, 12 pp.

Maslow, Abraham, *Motivation and Personality*. Harper & Row: New York, NY, 1954.

Maslow, Abraham, *Toward a Psychology of Being*. Van Nostrand: New York, NY, 1962.

Osborn, A.F., *Applied Imagination: Principles and Procedures of Creative Thinking* (revised edition). Charles Scribner's Sons: New York, NY, 1979.

Parnes, Sydney J., "Towards a Better Understanding of

Brainstorming," *The Creative Process,*Creative Education Foundation Press: Buffalo, NY, 1993.

Pfeffer, Jeffrey, "Power: The Not-So-Dirty Secret to Success in Organizations," *Stanford Business School Magazine,* March 1992, pp. 10-15.

Pritchett, Price, *New Work Habits for a Radically Changing World.* Pritchett & Associates, Inc.: Dallas, TX, 1994.

Ray, Michael, and Myers, Rochelle, *Creativity in Business.* Doubleday & Company, Inc.: Garden City, NY, 1986.

Rehner, Jan, *Practical Strategies for Critical Thinking.* Houghton Mifflin Company: Boston, MA, 1994.

Russell, Peter, *The Brain Book.* E.P. Dutton: New York, NY, 1979.

Slabbert, Johannes A., "Creativity in Education Revisited: Reflection in Aid of Progression," *Journal of Creative Behavior,* Vol. 28, No. 1, pp. 60-69.

Solomon, C.M., "What an Idea: Creativity Training," *Personnel Journal,* Vol. 69, 1990, pp. 66-68, 70.

Solomon, Robert C., *Morality and the Good Life.* McGraw-Hill: New York, NY, 1984.

"Strive for Perfection—OR ELSE!," *Working Communicator,* Summer, 1992, p. 6.

Taylor, Paul W., *Principles of Ethics: An Introduction to Ethics.* Dickenson: Encino, CA, 1975.

Torrance, E.P. and Ball, O.E. (1984). *Torrance tests of creative thinking: Streamlined (revised) manual, figural A and B.* Scholastic Testing Service, Bensenville, IL.

Torrance, E.P. and Goff, Kathy (1989), "A Quiet Revolution," *Journal of Creative Behavior,* Vol. 23, No. 2, pp. 136-145.

U.S. Department of Labor, *What Work Requires of Schools: A SCANS Report for America 2000,* Washington, D.C., 1991

Wise, R., "The Boom in Creativity Training," *Across the Board,* Vol. 28, 1991, pp. 38-40, 42, 65.

Wycoff, Joyce, *Mindmapping.* Berkley Books: New York, NY, 1991.

Ziglar, Zig, *See You at the Top.* Pelican Publishing Co.: Gretna, LA, 1980.